SUDDENLY VIRTUAL

SUDDENLY VIRTUAL

VIRTUAL

Making Remote Meetings Work

KARIN M. REED
JOSEPH A. ALLEN

Library of Congress Cataloging-in-Publication Data is Available:

ISBN 9781119793670 (Hardback)
ISBN 9781119793687 (ePub)
ISBN 9781119793694 (epdf)

COVER DESIGN: PAUL McCARTHY
COVER ART: © GETTY IMAGES | RLT_IMAGES
AUTHOR PHOTOS: COURTESY OF THE AUTHORS

SKY10024292_012521

For our families who allowed us to disappear into our writing to get this book quickly to our readers who are desperately seeking answers in this "Suddenly Virtual" world.

Joe: For Joy, Karen, Rachel, Alice, and Julia

Karin: For Shawn, Hayden, and Jackson

Contents

vii

Preface: The Collision and Convergence of Two Areas of Expertise

I n mid-March 2020, the world of work transformed before our eyes. While essential workers continued to valiantly do their jobs in the face of a global pandemic, the vast majority of corporate offices closed their brick-and-mortar locations and moved to entirely remote operations to protect the lives of their employees and loved ones. Suddenly, so-called knowledge workers were working from home, often in environments that were never designed for this new purpose. Important sales calls were taking place from the back porch. Training was being conducted virtually from dining room tables. Teams were navigating a dispersed workplace through the camera lenses of their home computers, smartphones, and tablets.

It was about a week before the "stay-at-home" orders swept across the United States that Dr. Joseph Allen and Karin Reed crossed paths. They were both working as subject matter experts for Logitech, the market leader in video collaboration tools, but they brought very different experiences and insights to the table.

Joe had been studying workplace meetings as an academic for over a decade, publishing more than 100 articles, book chapters, and books on the topic in academic outlets. He edited two volumes related to meeting science, including *The Cambridge Handbook of Meeting Science* and *Research on Managing Groups and Teams: Managing Meetings in Organizations*. As a recognized thought leader in this area, his work highlights the science-based best practices for workplace meetings. He provides consulting services for a variety of leaders and organizations toward the optimization of their workplace meetings.

Karin had been teaching on-camera communication skills for almost a decade through her communication training firm, Speaker Dynamics. After an Emmy-award winning career as a broadcast journalist and professional spokesperson, she developed a methodology to help business professionals be effective communicators when speaking to a camera, be it in the studio or in front of a laptop. Her first book, *On-Camera Coach: Tools and Techniques for Business Professionals in a Video-Driven World*, debuted as a #1 Hot New Release in Business Communications in 2017.

On March 11, 2020, Joe and Karin were asked to bring their expertise to bear as featured panelists for a Logitech webinar titled *Rethinking the Modern Meeting*. Little did they know how much the "modern meeting" would change within weeks, even within days of that early March webinar. The seismic shift would have broad implications for both of them – a veritable playground of new meeting science hypotheses to explore for Joe and an overnight explosion of business for Karin and her team from clients who were clamoring to get comfortable communicating by webcam alone.

The shift to virtual meetings was sudden and often traumatic for businesses across all industries. At first, rather than focusing on what would work best, businesses simply focused on what worked *now*. And what worked now was closing up the office and being suddenly virtual in nearly every meeting, often without the tools, the training, or the expertise to optimize the new "kitchen table" office. As weeks turned into months, though, businesses started to be more purposeful in the tools they used and the approach they took but still relied mostly upon gut feeling and perhaps trial and error.

All the while, Joe was researching and watching the evolution in real time and gathering the data that could inform decisions in the days, months, and years ahead. The move to remote work was having a profound and potent effect on our meetings and even our home life, and the findings were fascinating. In the meantime, Karin was delivering effective virtual communication training to thousands of people struggling to speak through that little lens embedded in their laptop or phone, when they wanted desperately to speak face-to-face but could not.

Months after that initial webinar on the modern meeting, Joe and Karin reconnected and realized their areas of expertise were powerfully colliding at a common pain point: making remote meetings work. Both Karin and Joe had been inundated with requests to help. While they felt truly fortunate to be able to answer many of those requests through training and consulting work, they knew they needed a way to amplify the message.

What if they brought together Joe's data-driven insights and Karin's real-world experiences to address a very pressing need the world over? The Meeting Scientist and the On-Camera Coach join forces again...ergo, *Suddenly Virtual: Making Remote Meetings Work.*

The Purpose of This Book

With so many relatively new virtual workers engaging in remote work and holding virtual meetings, science-based help to optimize the virtual meeting is not only needed but has also been fervently requested by those who are struggling to find a way to make these meetings work. Because there is so much uncertainty across the business landscape today, Joe and Karin hope this book can be a resource for as many people as possible in navigating virtual meetings where video is at their core.

With two very different but complementary skill sets, there are certain sections where Joe will take the lead and other sections where Karin will, as they each delve deeply into their respective areas of expertise. That's why in Sections 1–3, we will identify each chapter by labeling them "The Meeting Scientist Perspective" and "The On-Camera Coach Perspective" accordingly as they highlight new research insights springing from the rapid and exponential adoption of virtual meeting technology. However, their expertise fully converges for Sections 4–5 where they will speak in a unified voice as they discuss the problems, challenges, and pitfalls of meeting in this new modality with a look ahead at what the future of meetings may hold. Most important, throughout the book, they provide practical and actionable best practices that are backed by meeting research – practices that lead to more productive and effective virtual meetings that impact the bottom line.

How to Use This Book

This book is called a practical guide for a reason. It is designed to be a workbook that you can use to adopt and adapt your own ways of conducting business virtually. For that reason, they have included several tools for you to leverage that will help you build the capabilities of your own organization.

Checklists: Growth requires self-reflection. That's why they have provided checklists within and at the end of several chapters that you can use as an assessment tool of where you are now or a reminder of where you would like to be.

Try This: We often learn by doing, so in order to allow key takeaways to stick, they have included a few exercises for applying the techniques in your own environment and flexing your new skills.

Case Studies: This book is designed to provide you best practices steeped in solid science, but in order to see science come to life, it can be helpful to take a look at real-world examples. Starting with Section four, you will find case studies to illustrate how organizations across a variety of industries have adapted to the world of remote work.

They share what worked, what did not, and how they are charting their path to success in our suddenly virtual work environment.

Chapter Takeaways: Each chapter ends with a list of key takeaways to help you distill the content into digestible nuggets. Hopefully, you won't just read the book and place it on a shelf to gather dust. Rather, the hope is it becomes a frequent source of inspiration for many remote meetings to come. The bulleted lists, highlighting the essential points, are provided to serve as a quick reference.

Reflection Activity: In the final chapter, they will introduce the Adaptive Improvement Model (AIM) framework, which encourages you to consider things that you should *continue* doing, things you should *stop* doing, and things you should *start* doing. With your checklists and reflections from the book in hand, you can use the provided worksheet that will allow you to celebrate the things you are doing well while setting goals on things to do in the future. Thus, the book comes alive in your work life as you experiment with the practices and procedures discussed herein.

Ultimately, this book seeks to be a definitive guide for businesses looking to make their meetings as effective as possible in the ever-evolving "new normal" by leveraging the insights from some of the foremost thought leaders in meeting science and on-camera communication. Most businesses have settled into virtual meetings for the foreseeable future, and the decisions made in this arena will impact operations both now and in the times to come. The hope is the right decisions will be easier to make after you finish reading this book.

Acknowledgments

A very special thank-you goes out to our technical writer, Camie Schaefer, whose edits, thoughts, and input were essential for making our volume consistent and meaningful. We are grateful to Joe's research manager, Emilee Eden, for her assistance with identifying and sourcing references and citations. We express appreciation to both our beta readers, Joy Allen and Kristin Bair, for their insightful comments and ideas for enhancing the manuscript for our eventual readers. Additional thanks to those who so willingly shared their expertise, insight, and anecdotes: Massimo Rapparini, Scott Wharton, Matthieu Beucher, Charles Kergaravat, Kori Christensen, Dan Hawkins, Bridget Fletcher, Michael Shehane, Karen Hills, Christine Vucinich, and Shannon Heath. By sharing your stories, you helped all of us to better understand our suddenly virtual world and what the future may hold.

PART ONE

Our New Virtual Reality – A Suddenly Remote Workforce

Think back to October 2019. Now imagine what your work life looked like at that time. Maybe you hated your long commute and tried not to tally up the annual hours spent getting to and from the office. Perhaps you actually enjoyed flying to meet with potential customers in far-flung places and taking in the sights of an unexplored city. Or were you like so many of us who planned to revolt if we had to sit through one more pointless meeting in that cramped conference room, with coworkers who all watched the clock eat up time that could be spent "getting stuff done"? Oh, what a difference just a few months can make.

In this section, we reflect on the new reality introduced to the world of business by the COVID-19 pandemic. We begin with Joe, who describes what happened to work and more specifically, to the work meeting (Chapter 1). We then hear from Karin, who focuses on the hopeful truth that videoconferencing is a viable substitute for face-to-face meetings. She delves into its rapid adoption across corporate America as well as the value that video communication can bring when the world becomes remote (Chapter 2).

QUICK WARNING: If you flipped right past the preface, we would suggest you flip back and give it a read. Not only does it explain why a meeting scientist and an on-camera coach are collaborators in the first place, but it also tells you how to get the most out of this book by laying out the structure, the tools, and the opportunity to make it a working document. Don't worry, we'll wait.

Chapter 1

What Happened to Meetings?

The Meeting Scientist Perspective

Perhaps an important question to ask is "When did the world change?" Certainly, the world changed quickly, and many workers were either without work or found themselves in a dramatically different work environment. While the change was nearly instantaneous for some, others experienced a more gradual progression as the world tried to navigate the uncharted territory of a global pandemic. The facts on the ground shifted – not just day by day, but also hour by hour. A universal sense of uncertainty bled into every aspect of our lives.

The business world sought to adapt to the changes, but in those early days, ever-changing information meant that plans were scrapped almost as soon as they were written.

In this chapter, we will explore:

- The sequence of events that led to much of the world of work going remote.
- The rise of the virtual meeting.
- How businesses scrambled to adapt to the new virtual reality.

How Did We Get Here?

When did you first really pay attention to what was happening with COVID-19? From your current vantage point, you may find it hard to believe that most of us did not give it a whole lot of thought when it first reared its ugly head in China. Few of us could have imagined then how it would soon turn our world upside down. However, you probably do remember a watershed moment which signaled a shift in mindset. Maybe it was the cancellation of the NBA season or the closure of your college campuses? That's when we were suddenly glued to the TV and felt like we could not keep up with the news or the changes swiftly overtaking every aspect of our lives. The pandemic was a force to be reckoned with, and no one was going to be left unimpacted.

To put what happened to work and workplace meetings into proper context, here's a quick timeline of events.

Timeline of Events from the COVID-19 Pandemic (Kantis, Kiernan, and Bardi 2020)

December 8, 2019	A patient in the city of Wuhan sought medical help for pneumonia-like symptoms.
January 3, 2020	China officially notifies the WHO of an outbreak.
January 21, 2020	United States confirms its first case in Washington state, a man who traveled to the Wuhan area.
January 23, 2020	WHO meets again and decides not to declare the outbreak a Public Health Emergency of International Concern (PHEIC).

January 24, 2020	Nepal, Vietnam, France, and Malaysia confirm their first cases. Wuhan construction crews are working on two hospitals to treat patients of the outbreak: the first is to be completed on February 3 and the second in early February.
February 4, 2020	The U.S. Food and Drug Administration issues an emergency use authorization for CDC's diagnostic test. President Trump pledges to safeguard Americans from the coronavirus in his State of the Union address.
February 7, 2020	Total Cases Confirmed Globally: 31,484.
February 10, 2020	The United Kingdom declares that the coronavirus constitutes a serious and imminent threat to public health. The Trump administration releases a budget proposal for FY21 that would sharply cut funding for WHO and global health funding.
February 13, 2020	U.S. CDC Director says that the coronavirus will likely become a community virus and remain beyond this season.
February 15, 2020	The United States announces plans to evacuate nearly four hundred Americans quarantined on the Diamond Princess cruise ship; passengers who test positive for COVID-19 will be treated in Japan.
February 25, 2020	U.S. CDC warns that spread to the United States is likely and that people should prepare.
February 29, 2020	Australia reports its first death, an evacuee from the Diamond Princess. The United States reports its first death, a man in his fifties with an underlying health condition. Washington state declares a state of emergency.
March 7, 2020	Roughly 5,861 coronavirus tests are completed by CDC and public health labs in the United States. New York declares a state of emergency.

March 11, 2020	WHO declares the coronavirus outbreak a pandemic. Washington, D.C., declares a state of emergency. United States announces level 3 travel advisory and suspends entry to all foreign nationals traveling from China, Iran, and certain European countries at any point during the 14 days prior to their scheduled travel to the U.S. NBA suspends their season. Italy closes all shops and venues across the country. The United Nations reports that about 20% of students are out of school globally as a result of the pandemic.
March 12, 2020	U.S. stocks record their worst day since 1987. New York City declares a state of emergency. Ohio closes all public schools until at least April 3, 2020. France closes all schools. Virginia declares a state of emergency.

As of the writing of this book, more than 81 million people have been infected and over 1.8 million have died from the pandemic worldwide. Cases occurred in 188 countries, with many of them seeing their citizens dying from this disease.

The public health response has varied from country to country, with some shutting down immediately and asking citizens to stay home for weeks (e.g. South Korea) and others simply waiting for herd immunity to be achieved (e.g. Sweden). In the United States and many other countries the world over, the pandemic shut down the economy, the schools, and our favorite restaurants. Essential workers (e.g. some in manufacturing and many in grocery stores, farms, meat-packing, and so on) carried on in their work to feed the population, and so also carried the initial brunt of the burden of the disease.

As this happened, teachers learned how to go fully online, parents learned how to teach kids from home, and many organizations required their employees to work remotely. The kitchen table, bedroom, back porch, or home office became many people's only office. Demand for computers, webcams, headsets, desks, standing desks, monitors, and even "desk treadmills" skyrocketed, making some firms scramble to deal with supply, and with some individuals waiting for weeks for key tools they needed to go fully remote.

For years, organizations danced around the work-from-home issue. Some workers who sought the flexibility of a work-from-home life were denied time and again. Flexible work schedules were a niche area in academic research and even more niche in the actual workplace. Then, COVID-19 hit, and everyone was "suddenly virtual." The organizational sciences refer to this event as an equilibrium shift. Although the world had its challenges in October 2019, the economies were humming along at what might be called equilibrium. Then, a sudden and deep shock to the system occurred and fully unfolded over the following few months. In psychology, key events in one's life might be considered flashbulb moments, such as, in the past, "Where were you when Neil Armstrong landed on the moon?" or "Where were you on 9/11?" Now, we have, "Where were you during the COVID-19 pandemic?"

Like so many knowledge workers, Karin's office became a time capsule of March 2020, with sticky notes on the wall reflecting to-do lists for projects that were either scrapped or put on hold until a later date. One particularly poignant email from that time from Karin to a client read in part, "Let's reschedule the workshop for June. Surely things will be back to normal by then." Hindsight, of course, reveals the level of denial or even folly in those words. Even at the end of 2020, attempting to reschedule large group trainings seems ill-conceived. Luckily, Karin already had been delivering a third of her training virtually for years, but with COVID-19, that third became 100% of her business practically overnight.

Big events such as these flashbulb moments or lengthy world events (e.g. World War I, World War II, etc.) usually mean big changes. And these big changes usually have a lasting effect. For example, following the events of September 11, 2001, in the United States, the experience of getting on a plane in the U.S. changed forever with long lines for screening passengers, waiting areas forbidden for all but those who held tickets, and shoes removed while screening, among other things. Changes like these sometimes last in the name of safety, while others may remain out of convenience or cost savings. If you are in commercial real estate, consider this your warning. Remote work and the virtual office are big changes caused by a big event that will not be going away.

What Happened to Work?

Work changed for many. With the noted exceptions of many essential workers, the so-called "knowledge workers" were required to work differently. Instead of commutes and coffee at the corner shop, many began to roll out of bed, dress for success on the top half, make some passable coffee in a home brewing machine, and flip the laptop open for a long day of work from home. We would write our reports, crunch our numbers, take out the garbage, answer some email, fix our child's phone, deal with some urgent texts from a colleague, walk the dog, and log out an hour or two later than we did when we worked in the office. In fact, the average U.S. worker increased their hours worked per day by as much as three hours (Davis and Green 2020).

In this new work-from-home environment, we found ourselves no longer meeting with our colleagues face-to-face. The face-to-face meeting was banished and essentially vanished. Our video cameras came on, our cats started making cameos in our meetings, our children were now understood interruptions, and our pants became optional (hopefully unbeknownst to our colleagues). And with all of these elements of our new normal . . . the rise of the virtual meeting.

What Happened to Meetings?

Just prior to the pandemic in October 2019, Joe had the fortunate chance to collect data concerning virtual meetings with his colleagues at the University of Nebraska at Omaha. Although the data was limited to U.S. workers, its meaning increased dramatically as 2020 unfolded. In October 2019, nearly 80% of meetings were face-to-face, with less than 4% held over video. A little more than 13% of meetings were classified as hybrid, which refers to meetings where a couple of people may be in one conference room talking to folks in another conference room in another city, or country, via telephone or video conference. Thus, the vast majority of us essentially met face-to-face, be it in our office, our conference rooms, at our favorite coffee shops, restaurants, or even bars. As the bar graph below shows, things changed both dramatically and quickly.

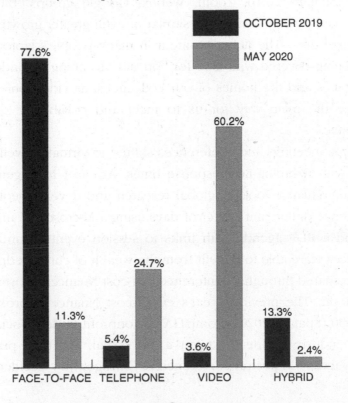

What Happened to Meetings?

After the onset of the pandemic, meetings became suddenly virtual. Workers experienced a 60% jump of meetings on video – almost 20 times the rate from before COVID-19. Telephone meetings jumped to nearly 25% of our meetings while face-to-face meetings were one-seventh its former total. In other words, we stopped meeting face-to-face, except in certain occupations deemed essential such as medical doctors, nurses, and other healthcare providers. However, even healthcare saw a rapid rise in telehealth. According to a survey by Sermo, an online physician network, 85% of physicians had adopted telehealth (typically video visits with patients), and 60% said they planned to continue using telehealth even after the pandemic is in the past (Wicklund 2020).

Unsurprisingly, videoconferencing software boomed. Total video calls in Microsoft Teams experienced 1000% growth in March 2020 alone (Spataro 2020). Zoom, Webex, Google groups, BlueJeans, Skype, and other software saw similar or even greater growth during that same time. The default camera in many people's laptops went from being covered with tape for "privacy" to being a window into our homes and the homes of our colleagues, as videoconferencing became the main way for us to meet and collaborate during a pandemic.

Large meetings and conferences shifted to virtual as well, sometimes with lightning-fast response times. Artificial Intelligence (AI) company Nuance took its global research and development (R&D) conference online in a matter of days using a Microsoft Teams channel and a PDF agenda with links to session events. Hundreds of attendees were able to benefit from the wealth of cutting-edge information shared through a conference that cost Nuance almost nothing to put on. The previous year's event cost Nuance approximately $700,000 (Spataro 2020). CompTIA, a nonprofit trade association in the IT industry, made the pivot to all virtual. Ten days prior to a long-planned, in-person conference in Chicago, they decided to flip the switch and take it all online. The painstakingly prepared agenda, chock-full of working group meetings, speakers, sessions, and even a St. Patrick's Day celebration along the dyed-green Chicago River, was reworked for the new platform. And it worked – the virtual event attracted five times more people than were expected to attend the Chicago event, and CompTIA called the industry response to the conference "overwhelmingly positive" (Campbell 2020). The trend continued for months to come. Joe's professional conference, the Society for Industrial and Organizational Psychology (SIOP) conference, was online in June 2020, and the Interdisciplinary Network for Group Researchers (INGRoup) was online in October 2020.

Conclusion

Given our observations and the trends just identified, how we meet on a regular basis has changed, perhaps for good. Sure, COVID-19 will not last forever, but the tools used to collaborate during this time will continue to be available and a viable option for working remotely, working from home, and so on. Thus, in the following chapter, we acknowledge the truth: videoconferencing is a viable alternative for face-to-face meetings – and it works.

Chapter Takeaways

- The pandemic changed how many people work and how many people meet to collaborate and accomplish their jobs.
- The format for meetings switched from face-to-face being the dominant form to the virtual meeting, primarily video-based interaction.
- The short-term move to remote meetings will likely be part of a long-term impact – the way we meet will never be the same.

References

Campbell, Scott. 2020. "Canceled by COVID-19? Here's how to pivot your in-person meeting into a virtual success." *CompTIA* (blog). https://www.comptia.org/blog/how-in-person-virtual-event#.Xo9TPaSjnGA.linkedin.

Davis, Michelle F., and Jeff Green. 2020. "Three hours longer, the pandemic workday has obliterated work-life balance." *Bloomberg*. https://www.bloomberg.com/news/articles/2020-04-23/working-from-home-in-covid-era-means-three-more-hours-on-the-job.

Kantis, Caroline, Samantha Kiernan, and Jason Socrates Bardi. 2020. "UPDATED: Timeline of the Coronavirus." *Think Global Health*. Council on Foregin Relations. https://www.thinkglobalhealth.org/article/updated-timeline-coronavirus.

Spataro, Jared. 2020. "Remote work trend report: Meetings." *Microsoft 365* (blog). https://www.microsoft.com/en-us/microsoft-365/blog/2020/04/09/remote-work-trend-report-meetings/.

Wicklund, Eric. 2020. "COVID-19 gives providers a blueprint for new telehealth strategies." *mHealth Intellegence*. https://mhealthintelligence.com/features/covid-19-gives-providers-a-blueprint-for-new-telehealth-strategies.

Chapter 2

What Happened to Video Communication?

The On-Camera Coach Perspective

"How often do you turn your webcam on when in a virtual meeting?"

For years, Karin has asked that question at the beginning of count-less workshops focusing on effective virtual communication. Participants were given three options:

- Never
- Every time
- Only when I see everyone else doing it

For many years, the top answer was overwhelmingly the same – "never."

Since COVID-19 and the mass migration to video collaboration tools, Karin has trained thousands of people on speaking through a webcam, and that formerly popular answer has changed dramatically. Only a handful of those in the post–COVID-19 world respond that they never turn the camera on, and the number of people who turn the webcam on every time has steadily increased as the pandemic has worn on. However, the vast majority of workshop participants continue to opt for the third response: "Only when I see everyone else doing it." They are responding to peer pressure for good or ill and not to the sound science and practice that suggests turning on the camera.

This small window into the adoption of video as a core component of virtual meetings is telling and reflective of a larger trend. Yes, more people are turning on their webcams than ever before, but there are still some barriers to adoption that hold back universal usage.

In this chapter, we will explore:

- How video became a viable alternative to face-to-face interactions.
- What value video brings to virtual meetings.
- How video impacts remote workers.
- Why video can be a critical element in meetings with external stakeholders.

Paving the Way for Virtual Video Communication

Video chat and collaboration did not arrive with COVID-19. Rather, the earliest form of video chat appeared in 1927, when AT&T's Bell Labs debuted technology that would allow speakers to see someone in real time on a phone call. The one-way TV demo call between then–Commerce Secretary Herbert Hoover and AT&T's President Walter Gifford sparked fascination but did not pave the way to public use, mainly due to a lack of network infrastructure.

In 1964, AT&T broke ground again with the introduction of the Picturephone at the World's Fair in New York City to much fanfare. However, a small-scale rollout of the technology in 1970 did not gain the necessary momentum to make the Picturephone commercially viable. Attempts in the 1980s yielded the same results. The market was still reticent to shift from a traditional phone call to a video one, seemingly dooming video phones to a fate of failed innovation (Uenuma 2020).

It was only when the platform for video calls moved from phone lines to the Internet that video communication began to gain a foothold. In 1993, a University of Cambridge scientist connected a camera to the Web in an effort to monitor the department's coffee pot levels. He and his fellow scientists could check on those pots regularly online, which they did. However, to his great surprise, many other people did, too. His coffee pot cam in essence went viral (Kesby 2012).

The coffee pot cam could arguably be the genesis for a deluge of video communication innovation. Commercial webcams hit the marketplace. The "watery bloop" of a Skype call with its accompanying techno music became a familiar soundtrack for PC users in the early 2000s. But the real game-changer was FaceTime on Apple's iPhone 4 in 2010, which prompted an endless string of software developers to create video-based platforms for various mobile devices as well as desktops and laptops that normalized virtual video communication for the masses.

FaceTime and its cousins primed the pump for what would be one of the most extraordinary shifts in our history in the way we meet and conduct business communication.

Stay at Home becomes "Stay on Zoom"

In early April 2020, more than 90% of the population of the United States was under local or state "stay-at-home" orders (Chavez, Hanna, and Maxouris 2020). With face-to-face interactions out of the question for large swaths of the nation, people were hungry for ways to connect both professionally and personally.

In the early days of the lockdown, the focus was mostly on finding ways to connect with friends and family, and the quest largely ended with Zoom. The video meeting app was the number-one free videoconferencing app on Apple's app store and experienced a 300% growth in daily usage by April 1 compared to the time before stay-at-home orders (Bary 2020). In just the first three weeks of April alone, Zoom added 100 million participants (Uenuma 2020).

Suddenly birthday parties, bridal showers, and book clubs were taking place on Zoom and other video platforms. While it couldn't provide an exact replica of an in-person experience, it was pretty darn close, and the price was right – free. Besides which, the technology was relatively easy and usable even for those who had never used videoconferencing before. Lack of familiarity is one of the biggest barriers to adoption for any technology, and with so many people staying at home and staying on Zoom for all manner of reasons, people became more comfortable navigating the relatively intuitive interface in order to stay close but socially distanced in their personal lives.

In the workplace, though, Zoom had plenty of videoconferencing competition that was often already well-established, if not utilized at high levels across the enterprise. WebEx, BlueJeans, GoToMeeting, and Microsoft Teams, along with many others, had established a strong presence in corporate America. However, many remote workers spoke of using the corporate platform when they had to but also of using a personal Zoom account when allowed by company policy. Some companies even found themselves using different platforms based upon the use case, for example, Zoom for training and Microsoft Teams for internal meetings, or WebEx for sales calls and Adobe Connect for internal presentations. This mix-and-match of multiple platforms presented its own challenges, which we will address in Chapter 12. Regardless of the software of choice, video communication had come into its own and opened up the eyes of new users to the benefits it could bring.

The Value of Video in a Virtual Meeting

Prior to the pandemic, the majority of the world was not a "webcam-on" culture, even for those teams which were dispersed and worked remotely. While some organizations made it mandatory for employees to use video in virtual meetings, most left it up to the individual user to decide whether to have their camera on or off. It was not uncommon for duct tape or a sticky note to be placed strategically over the lenses of the built-in cameras on laptops. Certain laptops already came with shutters that could be slipped over their built-in cameras for privacy purposes – one more layer of protection against appearing unexpectedly on camera. Most people never expected, nor wanted, to be on camera.

The pandemic in essence ripped off the Band-aid (or the duct tape) of webcam usage. Once face-to-face interactions became off-limits, most people begrudgingly started turning their video on during corporate meetings, if only because they were told to give it a try. Soon enough, many video conference converts (by choice or by force) started to find the value that video can bring to virtual meetings.

Deeper Connection

Whether extroverted or introverted, humans are social beings. Taking away our ability to see others chips away at the very core of who we are, and strict social distancing can feel almost cruel to those who thrive on interpersonal contact. No wonder rates of depression have skyrocketed since the pandemic began. For humans, social interaction and social connection are understood as a core human need and the desire to connect is a fundamental drive (Baumeister and Leary 1995). Without it, humans experience distress, children experience developmental delays, loneliness creeps in, and adverse outcomes (e.g. aging, cardiovascular health risk, suicide, and mortality in general) become more common (Hawkley and Cacioppo 2010).

Sure, a telephone call helps to lessen those feelings of withdrawal and isolation, but being able to see someone's face, even on a screen, adds a layer of connection that audio alone can't provide.

Video incorporated into virtual communication allows for a much deeper connection than what you can create with a disembodied voice. This is especially true if your relationship with that conversation partner was not fully formed and sufficiently built upon shared in-person experiences in the first place. If you know someone well, a phone call with that person can feel very personal and satisfying, but that may be at least partially due to the fact that your mind can fill in the gaps of what you can't see. While chatting, you may be visualizing that person's likely body language and facial expressions, all of which gives you a much fuller experience than if you were talking to someone on the phone whom you do not know well. Perhaps you've never even met this person before. You can't fill in the gaps and achieve that satisfying deep connection because you don't have enough backstory to do so.

For those remote meetings where you are not intimately familiar with your fellow attendees, video is invaluable in creating connections that make the interaction impactful. If someone can see you speaking, you have humanized the message and made it much more likely to be remembered. Meeting research supports this idea via media richness theory (Dennis and Kinney 1998). It argues that as we receive more cues as recipients of a message across a given medium, the amount of potential information that can be transferred increases, as does the effectiveness of the communication itself. Not turning video on when meeting in a virtual environment removes one of the most powerful tools you have in conveying your message well.

Better Accountability

Think back to your most recent conference call. Perhaps you had your phone on speaker and were focused intently on what was being discussed, or perhaps you had your phone on mute so your team-mates could not hear you typing away on your keyboard as you answered your emails.

One of the biggest challenges of an audio-only meeting is the gravitational pull of multitasking. In fact, research conducted by Inter-call, a large conference call company, found that 65% of conference call attendees are "doing other work" during those virtual meetings that are audio alone (Angle 2020). And why not? After all, we are only required to use our ears, not our eyes, right? You can easily listen in while ticking off a whole host of items on your to-do list at the same time. Unfortunately, as much as we want to believe that we are master multitaskers, research indicates that this does not line up with reality. Our productivity suffers, as do the outcomes of our meetings.

If your virtual meeting involves everyone turning their webcams on, the lens holds people accountable. It sees everything, and as much as you try to hide checking out that incoming text or your sur-reptitious search for a birthday gift for your Aunt Alice, your cowork-ers can see that you are not giving the meeting your undivided attention. Expect to be called out.

The benefits of having the webcam on were witnessed by Srini Koushik, Chief Technology Officer of Magellan Health, who was quoted in the 2017 Forbes Insights report, *The Connected Culture*: "Once video engages during a call, the entire feel and etiquette of the meeting changes. Participants are less apt to 'zone out.' The result is a superior level of closeness and engagement" (Forbes Insights 2017).

From a meeting science perspective, most of the multitasking behaviors just mentioned would be labeled counterproductive meet-ing behaviors or counterproductive use of technology in meetings (Allen, Yoerger, and Lehmann-Willenbrock 2015; Brown et al. 2016). These behaviors range from simple bad behavior while engaged in the meeting (e.g. complaining or blaming) to the distracting behav-iors (e.g. texting, emailing, shopping, etc.), and all of them are known to harm overall meeting satisfaction, effectiveness, and performance. Furthermore, they can even sow distrust among colleagues because being disengaged in the meeting (say, completing your online grocery order) means a colleague expecting your support could be left out on a limb with an idea they proposed.

Body Language Has a Voice

We do not communicate through words and vocal production alone. We communicate with our whole bodies – our facial expressions, our posture, and the way we position ourselves relative to our conversation partners. We won't enter into the controversial fray of how much our body language is responsible for communicating the message, but suffice it to say that various studies have suggested nonverbal communication could account for anywhere from 55% to over 90% of how we communicate a message. Without a doubt, body language provides important clues into the meaning of the message we are conveying, and a lack of those visual clues creates a rather large void in our understanding of intent and impact.

Imagine you are conducting a virtual meeting with video off. You state what you consider to be a key point and appropriately wait for a response from your audience. What you hear is silence. What does that mean? Does that silence indicate that they are in total agreement with what you just said, or does it mean that they are confused, in total disagreement, or simply not listening to you at all? Without video, you have no way of knowing unless you specifically poll the room by asking each person to weigh in verbally. You may want to do this anyway, but wouldn't it be easier to begin that process by actually reading those nonverbal cues revealed in the video boxes on screen? If someone is nodding along, you know where that person stands. If someone is looking perplexed with a furrowed brow, then it might be wise to lean into that visual cue and ask him or her to speak up.

By the same token, if you are seen on screen delivering a message, your body language will enhance your ability to communicate authentically and your audience can more easily read your intent. We all know how tone is so difficult to read in an email or text. A spoken message at least allows you to read tonality, but the richest modality of delivery where your audience can hear and see you communicate leaves less room for misunderstanding.

The Value of Video for Internal Meetings

The culture shock was real for colocated teammates who were suddenly tossed to the winds and landed in their homes at the beginning of the pandemic. For those newly dispersed teams, video became a critical component for team cohesion, allowing coworkers to still interact with their officemates in a meaningful way. And yes, there is meaning in a virtual happy hour. But the benefits of video communication, especially for remote teams, had already been well-documented and recognized by organizations that had been operating in that modality for years.

Better Team Performance

A fall 2019 Forbes Insights survey of more than 300 executives revealed just how valuable video is for teams that span the globe. High-quality video collaboration tools allow the "best and brightest" to work seamlessly on a project no matter where they are in the world. Consider the words of Brett Durnell, a manager of Unified Communications at F5 Networks, a true believer in leveraging video for global teamwork: "We have international meetings where there can be ten different faces on the screen all working together as if they were in the same room. It changes the nature of the meeting, making it more engaging, fun, and collaborative."

The survey results also revealed that at least 70% of respondents found that video meetings help drive the engagement of remote workers, improve team effectiveness, and enable individuals to be more productive. Keep in mind, this survey was conducted in the fall of 2019 prior to the bulk of business taking place virtually. As Joe found through his research, the benefits of video have been even more pronounced since the pandemic took hold, with even an over-correction in productivity. Many employees who had never *not* had a commute found it hard to clock out when work was only a room or even an arm's-length away, represented by a laptop sitting on a kitchen table (Green 2020). The fear of burnout was based in solid science, and corporations even today are wrestling with strategies to keep their employees from succumbing to it (Torman 2020).

The Video Portal: A Window into Our Coworkers' Homes

One of the more intriguing aspects of video meetings for suddenly remote teams was the opportunity to see our coworkers in a whole new light due to our ability to see them in a whole new environment. Admit it. You spent way too much time obsessing over someone's cool kitchen or what appeared to be a world-class collection of bob-bleheads lined up on a bookshelf in the background.

At the workplace, we tend to define our teammates mainly by their roles in the organization, and we view them through that prism. After all, our interactions with them are mainly professional, with perhaps a handful of relationships that go below the surface.

That curated veneer was stripped away to some degree by the video portal created by the reliance upon virtual communication. Not only did it afford the opportunity to check out everyone's space outside of the office, but it also allowed us to see our coworkers as whole people rather than just their roles. Who knew that Brenda has a green thumb with a penchant for orchids or that Chris collects beer cans from all over the world and displays them in alphabetical order on built-in shelves crafted for that purpose?

We also met their children, their pets, their significant others, and their roommates in a way that felt simultaneously refreshing and invasive. What made it okay was the fact that everyone was in the same situation. One of the early suggestions to newly remote workers was to give context to your work-from-home space – let everyone know the unique challenges you face to create understanding. Knowing what each person was dealing with in this new virtual environment led to less eye-rolling and more empathy. If someone suddenly muted their audio during a video meeting, perhaps it was because their elderly dog who refused to sit more than two feet from his master started to snore at a decibel that was untenable. Technical challenges might be attributed to bandwidth creaking under the weight of two adults simultaneously conducting virtual meetings, while their two little ones tried to navigate online school.

Psychological science backs the interesting benefits and occasional drawbacks of this new level of familiarity. The research is pretty clear that familiarity with others breeds liking, empathy, compassion, attraction, but also occasional contempt (e.g. a Red Sox fan disheartened to realize his coworker is a diehard Yankees fan) (Curtis, Rhoades, and Waguespack Jr 2012; Zagefka, Noor, and Brown 2013; Rindfleisch and Inman 1998). In one study, researchers found that knowledge of disaster areas increased willingness to donate, suggesting that familiarity bred compassion behavior. While the adage states that to know a person, one must walk a mile in their shoes, perhaps getting a glimpse of their book collection will suffice in helping us understand them a bit more.

In so many ways, we were all in this together, and the impacts on relationships with our coworkers are still being evaluated and analyzed today.

The Value of Video for External Meetings

Perhaps no team within an organization was more deeply affected by the stay-at-home dictates than the sales force. While some companies were exclusively selling virtually, most were not, and that pivot for some organizations felt akin to turning a giant cruise ship. It can be done but not without a lot of effort and forethought. Sales folks, by their very nature, crave face-to-face interaction. Without being able to begin a sales call with a handshake, what was the best alternative?

The Virtual Sales Call

Since the pandemic began, almost 90% of business-to-business (B2B) sales have moved to a remote model, whether that be videoconferencing or phone. Certain sectors – technology, media, and telecom especially – are leading the way, but according to McKinsey, "Sales leaders are already moving quickly to navigate the crisis, with the best ones focusing on how to make targeted changes that help their businesses weather the storm and start preparing for the recovery" (Gavin et al. 2020).

While digital sales channels (think mobile apps, social media channels, and online communities) are gaining in importance, the person-to-person experience is still one of the cornerstones of sales strategy. COVID-19 forced sales leaders to determine what that would look like in the new normal. For many organizations, person-to-person became video-image-to-video-image, and they were pleasantly surprised by the results and the impact on the bottom line. According to Gong, the #1 remote sales platform, prior to the pandemic, 41% more deals were won when the webcam was on during virtual sales calls, which is unsurprising, considering what a video-enabled meeting offers. Video humanizes the message, allows you to deeply connect and build and foster relationships – all powerful tools in any sales strategy (Orlob 2019).

While some organizations are just dipping their toes into using video on sales calls, other companies are going beyond real-time videoconferencing and embracing asynchronous video for email outreach. Platforms like BombBomb and Vidyard allow sales professionals to create personalized videos to send out to prospects. With shifts in how humans consume information, betting on video to cut through the noise seems like a pretty safe bet. Research by Wyzowl, a video marketing firm, shows that 66% of consumers prefer watching a video to reading about a product (Santora 2020). Video in an email is surely a differentiator from the typical text-only (PDF attached) version, and it delivers a message in a way that most people prefer.

The exploration of new ways of selling came at a critical time for many businesses. For example, in the pharmaceutical and biotechnology industries, product launches planned for years needed to be mapped out using virtual strategies never imagined prior to the pandemic. Savvy sales leaders recognized that their sales forces needed to be equally as competent and confident on camera as they were in person because their go-to market strategy might be completely virtual, totally in-person, or a combination of the two.

Those who try to wait it out for a return to "normalcy" do so at their own peril. According to McKinsey, "B2B sales operations going forward will look fundamentally different from what they were before the pandemic." With video as a core component of the sales process, best-in-class organizations are moving to create best-in-class virtual communicators and investing in the technology and training to stand out (Gavin et al. 2020).

Conclusion

By June 2020, videoconferencing had been fully embraced and entrenched in corporate America. According to a survey conducted by Demand Metric in the spring of that year, 95% of respondents reported using video meetings regularly for work, with 87% of them saying they use it more than ever before. However, the accelerated adoption due to work from home, travel restrictions, and social distancing has not been without some speedbumps (Metric 2020).

A full 94% of those who were engaging in virtual video meetings encountered barriers in using the tools effectively. The top three were video quality issues, video call fatigue, and technical issues (with keeping people's attention a close fourth). Furthermore, even if they manage to overcome the barriers, very few people have been trained on how to optimize those meetings. As it turns out, following meeting science and video communication best practices can go a long way in making virtual meetings work. We will look at both in Section 2 (The Meeting Scientist Perspective) and Section 3 (The On-Camera Coach Perspective).

Chapter Takeaways

- As the nation responded to the pandemic, "Stay at Home" largely became "Stay on Zoom" with the video meeting app rising to number one on Apple's app store for free videoconferencing options by early April 2020.

- Broad usage of personal video chat leads to explosive adoption of video collaboration tools in the workplace, with a variety of platforms being used, often simultaneously, within organizations.

- With a shift toward a "webcam-on" culture, businesses begin to see the benefits of video in virtual meetings – the potential to form deeper connections, less opportunity for participants to multitask, and the ability to read body language to develop a clearer understanding of the intent and impact of messages being conveyed.

- Video meetings are enhancing team cohesion, performance, and productivity while also reshaping the way coworkers view each other.

- No longer are teammates defined by just their roles; the video portal created by "work from home" provided a fuller picture of their coworkers.

- Video is a core component of virtual sales strategy as organizations seek new ways to build relationships, humanize their messages, and take the anonymity out of a sales process that used to rely upon face-to-face interactions.

References

Allen, Joseph, Michael Yoerger, and Johanna Jones Lehmann-Willenbrock. 2015. "Would you please stop that!?: The relationship between counterproductive meeting behaviors, employee voice, and trust." *Journal of Management Development* 34 (10): 1272–1287.

Angle, Keane. 2020. "Working from home? Overcome audience attention spans with these virtual presentation tips." Deliverable Coaching.com. https://www.deliverablecoaching.com/post/working-from-home-overcome-audience-attention-spans-with-these-virtual-presentation-tips.

Bary, Emily. 2020. "Zoom, Microsoft Teams usage are rocketing during coronavirus pandemic, new data show." *MarketWatch*. https://www.marketwatch.com/story/zoom-microsoft-cloud-usage-are-rocketing-during-coronavirus-pandemic-new-data-show-2020-03-30.

Baumeister, Roy F., and Mark R. Leary. 1995. "The need to belong: Desire for interpersonal attachments as a fundamental human motivation." *Psychological Bulletin* 117 (3): 497–529.

Brown, D., M. A. Yoerger, J. D. Crowe, and J. A. Allen. 2016. "The impact of counterproductive meetings behaviors on burnout, as moderated by Coworker Trust." Midwestern Psychological Association Conference, Chicago, IL.

Chavez, Nicole, Jason Hanna, and Christina Maxouris. 2020. "Nearly all Americans are under stay at home orders but Fauci says the US needs more coronavirus restrictions." CNN online. https://www.cnn.com/2020/04/02/health/us-coronavirus-thursday/index.html.

Curtis, Tamilla, Dawna L Rhoades, and Blaise P Waguespack Jr. 2012. "Satisfaction with airline service quality: Familiarity breeds contempt." *International Journal of Aviation Management* 1 (4): 242–256.

Dennis, Alan R., and Susan T. Kinney. 1998. "Testing media richness theory in the new media: The effects of cues, feedback, and task equivocality." *Information systems research* 9 (3): 256–274.

Forbes Insights. 2017. "The connected culture: Unleashing the power of video in everyday collaboration." *Forbes Insights*. Forbes Media. https://i.forbesimg.com/forbesinsights/zoom/The_Connected_Culture.pdf.

Gavin, Ryan, Liz Harrison, Candace Lun Plotkin, Dennis Spillecke, and Jennifer Stanley. 2020. "The B2B digital inflection point: How sales have changed during COVID-19." McKinsey and Company. https://www.mckinsey.com/business-functions/marketing-and-sales/our-insights/the-b2b-digital-inflection-point-how-sales-have-changed-during-covid-19#.

Green, Jeff. 2020. "The pandemic workday is 48 minutes longer and has more meetings." *Bloomberg*. https://www.bloomberg.com/news/articles/2020-08-03/the-pandemic-workday-is-48-minutes-longer-and-has-more-meetings.

Hawkley, Louise C., and John T. Cacioppo. 2010. "Loneliness matters: A theoretical and empirical review of consequences and mechanisms." *Annals of Behavioral Medicine* 40 (2): 218–227.

Kesby, Rebecca. 2012. "How the world's first webacm made a coffee pot famous." BBC online. https://www.bbc.com/news/technology-20439301.

Metric, Demand. 2020. "The state of video in remote work 2020." Demand Metric. https://www.demandmetric.com/content/state-video-remote-work-2020.

Orlob, Chris. 2019. "10 tips for successful discovery calls in sales." *LinkedIn Sales Blog*. https://www.linkedin.com/business/sales/blog/b2b-sales/sales-opportunities-10-tips.

Rindfleisch, Aric, and Jeffrey Inman. 1998. "Explaining the familiarity-liking relationship: Mere exposure, information availability, or social desirability?" *Marketing Letters* 9 (1): 5-19.

Santora, Jacinda. 2020. "Video marketing statistics: What you must know for 2020." *Conversion Rate Optimization Blog*. https://optinmonster.com/video-marketing-statistics-what-you-must-know/.

Torman, Matt. 2020. "Forbes Insights: A video-first culture is critical for overcoming the workplace challenges of the future." *Zoom Blog*. https://blog.zoom.us/forbes-insights-video-first-culture-overcoming-workplace-challenges-of-the-future/.

Uenuma, Francine. 2020. "Video chat is helping us stay connected in lockdown. But the tech was once a 'spectacular flop'." *Time*. https://time.com/5834516/video-chat-zoom-history/.

Zagefka, Hanna, Masi Noor, and Rupert Brown. 2013. "Familiarity breeds compassion: Knowledge of disaster areas and willingness to donate money to disaster victims." *Applied Psychology* 62 (4): 640–654.

PART TWO

The Science of Meetings

M eeting science is a relatively young research area, with the
earliest studies that focused on the workplace meeting appearing less than 40 years ago (Schwartzman 1986). And yet so much of
our time as employees, managers, and leaders has been and continues to be wrapped up in this activity. In fact, prior to 2020, Joe
often referred to the exponential increase in workplace meetings as a
"meeting epidemic." That comparison is probably in poor taste given
the experiences of so many in 2020, but the fact remains that we
meet more now than ever before, with most workers seeing a 13%
increase in their overall meeting load (Bloomberg 2020).

In this section, Joe drives the discussion as he reviews meeting science from before the COVID-19 pandemic and our suddenly
virtual world. He provides checklists of counterproductive behaviors and best practices for effective meetings from the "old normal"
(Chapter 3). He then reveals some of the discoveries in meeting

science made since early 2020 – when everything changed – with another checklist and a reference guide for best practices for effective virtual meetings based upon the early research (Chapter 4). Video is an important part of those virtual meetings, but practices more specific to on-camera communication are discussed in Section 3.

Best Practices for Meetings Before COVID-19

The Meeting Scientist Perspective

"Hooray, I get to go to another meeting!"

Those words were likely never said by anyone. Rather, communal griping about meetings has been a feature of the corporate landscape since long before COVID-19. Prior to the pandemic, meetings in all their forms were common. More than 55 million meetings are held each day in the United States (Keith 2015). While the typical employee spends around six hours a week in meetings, the burden on managers is exponentially larger. Managers in larger organizations spend approximately 23 hours a week in meetings, and many spend up to 80% of their time in meetings or on meeting-related activities (Rogelberg, Scott, and Kello 2007).

With that much time spent in meetings, you have to wonder why we have not spent time improving them – or at least making meetings more tolerable. One possible answer can be found in the academic literature on meeting science: widespread inefficiency in workplace meetings. Current estimates indicate that upwards of half of all meetings are rated as "poor" by attendees. Not satisfactory. Not "okay." *Poor.* And this isn't just a qualitative problem. Further estimates suggest that organizations are wasting approximately $213 billion per year on ineffective, suboptimal, and/or poor meetings (Keith 2015). That's *billion* – with a "b."

In this chapter, we will explore:

- Some of the reasons we collectively do not enjoy most meetings.
- Best practices for what should occur before, during, and after a meeting.
- What should be expected of meeting leaders.
- What should be expected of meeting attendees.

It should be noted that most of the findings presented here are based primarily on face-to-face meetings. We will discuss to what degree these best practices still apply at the end of this chapter and in subsequent chapters.

Research Exposes Why People Dislike Many Meetings

Recent research sheds some light on why so many meetings receive a poor rating. For all of the grousing people do about meetings, it seems that the majority of problems stem from the attendees themselves – or, rather, from what are classified as counterproductive meeting behaviors. Researchers found not only that these behaviors are fairly common in meetings but that multiple counterproductive behaviors occur within a single meeting (Lehmann-Willenbrock, Allen, and Belyeu 2016; Yoerger et al. 2017).

Think about your last in-person meeting. Visualize the people in the room and how they interacted with each other. Now take a look at the table provided here. Consider indicating whether you recall seeing any of these behaviors.

Checklist of Counterproductive Meeting Behaviors in Last Meeting

Counter productive Meeting Behavior	Yes or No
1. Meeting attendees engage in long monologues that do not move the discussion forward.	[ ] Yes [ ] No
2. Meeting attendees go off the topic (e.g. talking about TV programs or other spare-time activities).	[ ] Yes [ ] No
3. Meeting attendees heavily criticize others in the meeting or others not present in the meeting.	[ ] Yes [ ] No
4. Meeting attendees use sarcasm to criticize others.	[ ] Yes [ ] No
5. Meeting attendees express resignation.	[ ] Yes [ ] No
6. Meeting attendees complain about things during the meeting.	[ ] Yes [ ] No
7. Meeting attendees use random sayings or empty phrases.	[ ] Yes [ ] No
8. Meeting attendees express little interest in trying out new ideas or procedures.	[ ] Yes [ ] No
9. Meeting attendees explain why everything has to stay the way it is.	[ ] Yes [ ] No
10. Meeting attendees shift responsibility to others or to management.	[ ] Yes [ ] No
11. Meeting attendees point out their work experience/expertise to show that they are superior.	[ ] Yes [ ] No
12. Meeting attendees occasionally leave the meeting.	[ ] Yes [ ] No
13. Meeting attendees arrive late to meetings.	[ ] Yes [ ] No
14. Meeting attendees leave the meeting early without giving a reason.	[ ] Yes [ ] No
15. Meeting attendees occupy themselves with things unrelated to the meeting (e.g. texting, emailing, etc.).	[ ] Yes [ ] No
16. Meeting attendees seem to let their minds wander during the meeting.	[ ] Yes [ ] No

Counter productive Meeting Behavior	Yes or No
17. Meeting attendees rarely participate in the meeting.	[ ] Yes [ ] No
18. Meeting attendees show obvious disinterest in the topics that are discussed.	[ ] Yes [ ] No
19. Meeting attendees express disinterest with their facial expression.	[ ] Yes [ ] No
20. Meeting attendees interrupt others.	[ ] Yes [ ] No
21. Meeting attendees try to be the center of attention in meetings.	[ ] Yes [ ] No
22. Meeting attendees are not interested in the views of the others.	[ ] Yes [ ] No
23. Meeting attendees make fun of other meeting attendees.	[ ] Yes [ ] No
24. Meeting attendees deliberately try to show up other meeting attendees.	[ ] Yes [ ] No
25. Meeting attendees intimidate other meeting attendees.	[ ] Yes [ ] No
TOTAL YES	[ ]

Now tally up your responses, keeping in mind that it is typical to see no fewer than five of those behaviors in a single meeting. Importantly, this checklist only captures the different types of behavior, not how often they occur. It is likely that multiple attendees engaged in counterproductive use of technology (e.g. texting, checking email, etc.). These behaviors are all problematic for a variety of reasons and can quickly become systemic.

Many of the best practices that we provide here help to eliminate these behaviors, in part because these practices increase meeting engagement. As people engage more in a meeting, we're less likely to hear people saying, "Sorry, I missed that, can you repeat the question?" This, as we all know, translates into "I was distracted by this cat video and totally missed the last three minutes of the meeting." Reducing counterproductive behaviors such as distraction encourages engagement and heightens meeting efficiency. Efficient meetings with engaged participants may lead to a faster accomplishment of meeting goals and may come with the bonus of ending a meeting early.

So, what can be done to make meetings worthwhile? The first step may well be to reframe how we perceive meetings. As Rogelberg et al. (2006) noted, many view meetings as interruptions in their flow at work, and so the first step in improving meetings is to make them places of refuge and opportunity rather than wells of lost time and energy. Fortunately, before COVID-19, scientific research on meetings had established many best practices.

Before-Meeting Best Practices

To make an effective meeting, several important things need to occur even before the meeting begins. Many may protest that their back-to-back meeting schedule leaves little time for solid preparation. However, we also know that one bad meeting can beget more meetings, if only to clean up the mess from the bad meeting. The science consistently notes that a little effort ahead of time will pay off with increased efficiency.

Meeting Design

One of the biggest before-meeting considerations is the proper design of the meeting. Before even scheduling or notifying folks of a meeting, one has to decide if a meeting is even necessary. Some would say the best meeting is a canceled meeting. Although a common sentiment, that's not going to work for the many collaborative processes that can only happen when we gather together. And that's the key. When deciding if a meeting is necessary, ask yourself the question,

"If we do not meet, can we move forward?" Usually, if someone needs something that they cannot access or achieve alone, a meeting may help move things forward. Thus, collaborative processes that require a meeting include, but are not limited to:

- decision-making
- problem-solving
- resource allocation
- obtaining information
- idea generation
- strategic planning, and so on.

After determining that a meeting is necessary, the meeting organizer has to decide first, how long the meeting needs to be and second, how many people to include in the meeting (Leach et al. 2009). The length of the meeting should fit the meeting goals. However, even with a long agenda, organizers should be mindful that long meetings are notoriously ineffective. If we schedule more time than is needed, we tend to fill the empty air and waste the remaining time. Thus, only schedule meetings for the length needed and *do not* let the default calendaring system decide it for you. If you believe you can get through the agenda and accomplish the goals in 20 minutes, then schedule the meeting for 20 minutes.

In terms of size, most people need to "right-size" their meetings – basically, a kind way of saying we need to make the meeting smaller. Smaller is typically better for collaborative processes, and five to seven attendees are generally the "sweet spot" for meeting size when decisions need to be made. Any larger than that and it gets hard for everyone to participate in a timely manner, limiting engagement and creating "wallflowers" within the otherwise productive meeting. If you encounter a wallflower (someone not participating), it may be because they are not key to the meeting, the meeting size is too large, or they have checked out. Right-size your meeting! Clip the wallflower and send them on their way to more productive uses of their time (Boivie et al. 2016). Additionally, make sure roles/tasks for the meeting are identified and assigned to the attendees (e.g. minutes, timekeeper, etc.).

The third thing to consider for meeting design is the meeting space and format needs. For face-to-face meetings, making sure the room is adequately sized for the meeting, has comfortable seating, and satisfies tech needs for presentations, if necessary. Prior to COVID-19, when considering virtual meetings, the general rule was to use the richest media possible. If you have a choice between videoconferencing and teleconferencing, always choose video. It should provide more cues for attendees to help with participation and interaction. For hybrid meetings, ensure that the face-to-face participants are aware of and attentive to their virtual counterparts. More will be said about the virtual components of design a bit later (Allison, Shuffler, and Wallace 2015), and a deeper dive into all of this will appear in subsequent chapters.

Pre-meeting Leader and Attendee Responsibilities

The success of the meeting is not the sole responsibility of the meeting leader. Quite the contrary. Both leader and attendee play vital roles in making the meeting productive even before it convenes. As we discussed in the design section, the leader or organizer must first set clear goals and identify desired outcomes for the meeting. However, this information does attendees no good if it's not shared ahead of time. Sharing offers attendees a chance to react and/or think about these things ahead of the meeting.

The second pre-meeting responsibility that is more leader-oriented is the agenda. Agenda usage is probably the most-prescribed meeting best practice. But, like most things, it's not the presence of the thing that matters, but how it is used. The agenda must be prepared ahead of time *and* circulated ahead of the meeting, thus enabling others to provide input and to prepare.

This leads us to the third and fourth pre-meeting responsibilities that are shared between meeting leaders and attendees: to ensure that the meeting is relevant to all invitees and that everyone comes having reviewed the agenda and understanding the goals and the desired outcomes (Cohen et al. 2011). Many who read this will balk at the fact that this will take time to implement. Who has time to prepare an agenda, circulate it, and review it before a meeting? Maybe you don't see the value of it and think "I can't even remember the last time I looked at a meeting agenda *before* the meeting." The fact that so many share these thoughts should be a big, bright, red flag. We are overbooked with meetings, and a good number of them would probably go away if we designed them properly (i.e. "Do I need this meeting?") and had better meetings (i.e. understanding that bad meetings beget more meetings).

Finally, it is essential to make sure your technology is working and ready to go. For face-to-face meetings, the technology might be computer connections, power cables, and projector. Technology can be checked by the meeting leader, organizer, or another designee. For virtual meetings, effort is needed across the entire attending group to check their own audio and video devices, their presentation materials, and so forth. Most of us hadn't put much thought into the video and audio quality of our built-in cameras and microphones on our laptops when we originally purchased them, but their adequacy or often inadequacy became readily apparent when virtual meetings became our only option for a time. This pre–COVID-19 best practice feels awfully timely now.

If all these best practices are implemented, including both design and responsibilities, the stage is set for an effective meeting. Without these practices in place, the stage is set regardless, but the suboptimal situation will ensure a less than effective meeting will occur. The issue is whether you want to enable the best possible chance for all the goals and outcomes to be accomplished *or* if you are prepared to put in the effort needed to overcome a less than ideal setup in terms of meeting efficiency.

During-Meeting Best Practices

And now the stage is set for showtime, with everyone prepared to collaborate and accomplish the stated goals and aims of the meeting. However, simply setting the stage and gathering is only the first step in making meetings effective. What happens *during* the meeting is equally if not more important than the preparation. And it is in the actual meeting itself that both the meeting leader and the attendees must engage in best practices for human interaction that enables the meeting to be effective. In spite of this, so many self-help books, quick-fix columns, and "best practice list" articles focus on what the leader must do. The good news for meeting leaders is that shared leadership in meetings is often the best strategy. If either side falls short, so will the outcomes of the meeting. That's why we are sharing best practices for both attendees and leaders.

One of Karin's recent clients, a large tech company, had enlisted her help for communication training. She was tasked with conducting a series of workshops for different teams throughout the organization, each of whom had a variety of roles and responsibilities. While the content was tweaked based upon how the techniques would be applied, what Karin hadn't accounted for was the need to dramatically tweak the timing of her sessions.

A noon start typically wound up being a 12:05 or even a 12:10 start. Breaks that were designed to be 10 minutes often went 15 minutes or more because attendees were slow to rejoin.

What she was told is that this was a reflection of the company culture that has a "loose relationship with the clock." She adjusted her timing with this in mind and built in a lot of flexibility for the inevitable delays.

But is this practice helping or hurting their organization? While several people did seem to arrive for the sessions on their own timing, others made a point of being punctual. Did everyone appreciate the grace period that was granted to those who were perpetually late, or did it secretly annoy those who stuck with the schedule?

During-Meeting Attendee Responsibilities

Karin's experience with that client highlights the challenges of upholding one of several responsibilities of meeting attendees. First, it is really, *really* important to arrive early (or on time). This is because early attendees can take advantage of pre-meeting talk, a form of informal communication that provides a space to catch up, interact socially, and even consider the reasons for the meeting. The research is clear that pre-meeting talk is essential (Allen, Lehmann-Willenbrock, and Landowski 2014). Further, research confirms that meetings that start late are anywhere between 10% to 50% worse than meetings that start on time (Allen, Lehmann-Willenbrock, and Rogelberg 2018). Attendees should arrive early, partake in a little pre-meeting talk, and not be the one to harm the overall meeting by being late.

Second, all those counterproductive meeting behaviors we opened this chapter with should be avoided. To reiterate, avoid complaining or dominating communication behavior (Kauffeld and Lehmann-Willenbrock 2012) as well as any activities that are unrelated to the meeting itself (e.g. texting). These behaviors, at minimum, distract the attendee from the purpose of the meeting and may even derail it entirely.

You might be thinking, "If I stop doing all those things, then what am I supposed to do during all my meetings?" Perhaps that thought was in jest or perhaps you can think of someone who might not have any other behaviors left in their repertoire if those are banned. But the third and perhaps most critical attendee responsibility is to engage and participate in the meeting. If we assume the design processes occurred, then attendees present were invited for a reason and not to be wallflowers. They are there to contribute, participate, and help accomplish the aims for which the meeting was called. Not only is it an attendee's job to participate, but it is also his or her job to encourage others to do likewise (Yoerger, Crowe, and Allen 2015).

During Meeting Leader Responsibilities

During the meeting, the leader's responsibilities parallel the expectations for attendees as well as the before-meeting best practices previously discussed. However, leaders have additional influence on how those best practices are implemented.

The meeting leader is responsible for ensuring the meeting starts on time (Rogelberg et al. 2014) and therefore must arrive early (or on time). Meeting lateness is a rampant problem, with nearly half of all meetings starting late (Allen, Lehmann-Willenbrock, and Rogelberg 2018). First, arriving early or on time may very well be one of the more important responsibilities of the leader. Second, just as the leader should have properly built the agenda prior to the meeting (i.e. with goals and outcomes, and perhaps time-stamps for the timekeeper), the leader is responsible for following the agenda. They should encourage everyone to participate.

Third, while everyone at the meeting is responsible for keeping the agenda on track, the leader has a larger role in minimizing counterproductive meeting behaviors. This includes avoiding distractions when they arise, minimizing multitasking behaviors of the entire group (Odermatt et al. 2018), and intervening when interpersonal communication patterns become dysfunctional. Sometimes the meeting can go off-topic when an attendee's comment becomes a monologue, the leader discusses frustrations with management, or any number of other complaining, blaming, or negative behaviors (for the full list, see the counterproductive checklist table at the beginning of this chapter). Research shows that procedural statements are an effective strategy to stop complaining or other inappropriate dialogue. Procedural statements might include things like "getting us back onto topic" or "let's parking-lot that idea" and focus on the task at hand" and similar processes. Interestingly, procedural statements can be used by the leader *or* by the attendee to politely transition back to the focus of the meeting or agenda item. The key is to make a procedural statement graciously, perhaps by even thanking the monologuer, or appreciating the complexity of the complaint, but ultimately pointing back to the meeting and its aims. Surprisingly, most attendees respond very well to procedural statements so long as there is a promise that topics important to them will be addressed at some future time.

Fourth, the meeting leader is responsible for closing down the meeting in a timely and effective manner. This includes ending on time, ensuring that minutes have been taken, and checking that all action items have been recorded and reiterated. One cannot overstate the importance of ending on time, as the end of the current meeting becomes an input to subsequent meetings. Many people have back-to-back meetings, and a late end to one meeting becomes a late start to the next meeting, thereby perpetuating the negative drain on meeting efficiency and effectiveness.

After-Meeting Best Practices

So, the meeting is over, and everyone leaves. What now? Well, meeting science has discovered several best practices that, if implemented, will essentially ensure the meeting has a lasting impact. There are also some long-term best practices that will enable all meetings to be more effective for individuals, teams, and organizations.

First, as soon as the meeting ends, the minutes should be finalized and shared along with any action items (Cohen et al. 2011). However, like with the agenda, action items are useless by themselves. They must be used correctly. For example, each action item should be assigned to an individual, and someone, perhaps the meeting leader or the minutes taker, must be responsible for following up. Oftentimes the follow-up occurs in subsequent meetings, but that may be a longer time interval than necessary, so having an assigned person to follow up on action items may actually move things along more quickly and make subsequent meetings more effective.

Second, and ideally before everyone departs, assess meeting satisfaction, effectiveness, and quality. Some interesting tech options have arrived on the scene for rating meetings and compiling information (e.g. MeetingScience). By briefly assessing meeting satisfaction, effectiveness, and quality, meeting leaders and attendees get immediate feedback and begin to seek ways to further improve their meetings. Ongoing feedback will go a long way toward highlighting areas for improvement, as well as identifying opportunities to celebrate the high-quality meetings that do happen from time to time and that will hopefully happen more frequently as best practices become just practices.

Third, with the recent meeting completed, meeting leaders and attendees should look at upcoming meetings. Are those routine meetings and any other meetings on the calendar really needed? If they are needed, then the best practices for before, during, and after the meeting should be implemented across the board to the degree that they are possible. This is especially important for routine meetings where the agenda can get stale and the meeting can become perfunctory rather than functionary. Consider a refresh of the agenda among other best practices.

Fourth, consider more long-term assessments. If meeting leaders and attendees notice that their organization does not evaluate the

45

satisfaction and effectiveness of meetings on the annual employee survey, then that needs to change. It's difficult, if not impossible, to change something when you don't know how you are doing in the first place. Assessing meetings annually would provide a baseline indication of how things are going, and if a best practices checklist was included in the survey, then the frequency of best practices could be assessed as well. This would give meeting leaders and attendees easy targets for improvement and optimization.

The Intuitive Nature of Meeting Science

Just guessing, but as you read the best practices in meeting science, you may have begun to think, "yeah, no duh." That's because meeting science is intuitive in many ways. In fact, some people would argue that most of the work Joe's done on meetings is common sense. Perhaps that's why he is so quick to mention simple facts: things like half of meetings start late and more than half of meetings are rated as poor, and so on. The problem with the intuitive nature of meeting science is that common sense continues to remain well . . . *uncommon.*

A Story from Joe's Perspective

Joe the scientist decided to become the subject of his research. Before engaging in a series of studies on meeting lateness, Joe decided to track his own meetings. Not the ones he organized, because those always started on time, but the ones he was required to attend. To his surprise, more than half of them were late. In many cases, the late start was caused by the leader arriving late and unprepared. In one particularly poignant experience, the meeting leader – a person a few levels up in the hierarchy of organization relative to Joe – arrived late and on the phone. The meeting leader proceeded to cup the phone and indicate they were going to run to the bathroom and be right back. Ten minutes passed. Twenty minutes passed. Thirty minutes passed.

Given the difference in the hierarchy of the institution, Joe could not just leave. Eventually, the leader came back to the room and started the meeting about 35 minutes past the start time. The agenda was clearly designed for an hour-long meeting, so after 20 minutes, the meeting leader said, "I think this is all important enough to keep us here, so let's proceed into the next hour." Joe's next meeting got bumped, along with those of the other attendees who found themselves scrambling to rework their schedules. And yes, if you were keeping track here, you've probably identified several counterproductive meeting behaviors happening here, and yes, the bad meeting did result in yet another meeting to clean up the mess.

Thankfully meeting experiences like that are not terribly common, but less problematic instances abound. In our observations, most meetings observed did up to half the best practices mentioned and *none* of them accomplished them all. As another thought experiment, here's a checklist of the best practices from meeting science discussed here. Think about a recent meeting you attended or led. Complete the checklist and see how many best practices were present. If your last meeting did them all, please contact Joe and tell him about it. His disbelief will be worth the phone call!

Checklist of Best Practices from Your Last Meeting

Best Practices for Meetings	Yes or No
Before	
1. Is it necessary to have this meeting?	[ ] Yes [ ] No
2. Does the meeting length fit the meeting goals?	[ ] Yes [ ] No
3. Is the meeting relevant to all attendees?	[ ] Yes [ ] No
4. Are roles/tasks for the meeting identified and assigned beforehand?	[ ] Yes [ ] No
5. Is the meeting format appropriate?	[ ] Yes [ ] No
6. Is the meeting space appropriate?	[ ] Yes [ ] No
7. Does the meeting space have functioning and needed technology?	[ ] Yes [ ] No

Best Practices for Meetings	Yes or No
8. Are meeting goals and outcomes clearly set?	[ ] Yes [ ] No
9. Is there a meeting agenda?	[ ] Yes [ ] No
10. Is the meeting information and/or document(s) sent with enough time for attendees to review?	[ ] Yes [ ] No
11. Are all attendees prepared for the meeting?	[ ] Yes [ ] No

During

1. Do meeting attendees arrive early or on time?	[ ] Yes [ ] No
2. Does the meeting leader arrive early?	[ ] Yes [ ] No
3. Is there pre-meeting talk?	[ ] Yes [ ] No
4. Does the meeting start on time?	[ ] Yes [ ] No
5. Does the meeting leader follow the agenda?	[ ] Yes [ ] No
6. Do attendees participate and engage in the meeting?	[ ] Yes [ ] No
7. Does the meeting leader encourage participation from all attendees?	[ ] Yes [ ] No
8. Do any attendees participate in counterproductive meeting behaviors (e.g. complaining, interrupting, etc.)?	[ ] Yes [ ] No
9. Does the meeting leader minimize any counterproductive meeting behaviors?	[ ] Yes [ ] No
10. Are procedural statements used by the leader or attendees?	[ ] Yes [ ] No
11. Does the meeting end on time?	[ ] Yes [ ] No

After

1. Do the meeting minutes get sent out immediately afterward?	[ ] Yes [ ] No
2. Are action items assigned to individuals?	[ ] Yes [ ] No
3. Is someone assigned to follow up on action items?	[ ] Yes [ ] No
4. Are meeting satisfaction, effectiveness, and/or quality assessed?	[ ] Yes [ ] No
5. Is there a feedback system for organizational meetings over time?	[ ] Yes [ ] No

TOTAL YES [＿＿＿＿＿]

Conclusion

As you reflect on your last meeting and the hopefully many best practices that were present, consider this question: Which of these best practices still apply in the virtual meeting world? Much to our surprise, nearly all of them are relevant in the virtual meeting format. In the next chapter, we delve into this realization and discuss new findings relative to best practices in the new virtual meeting world.

Chapter Takeaways

- Meetings are extremely prevalent in organizations in the pre–COVID-19 world, and most of them are in the face-to-face format.

- There are many different counterproductive meeting behaviors that are plaguing our meetings, making them less effective than they ought to be.

- Meeting science provides best practices for before, during, and after meetings that hold promise to both reduce counterproductive meeting behaviors and make our meetings efficient and effective.

- The checklists available here are useful, self-diagnostic tools that allow for immediate feedback and subsequent change.

- Meeting science best practices are intuitive, common sense, and uncommonly applied.

References

Allen, Joseph A., Nale Lehmann-Willenbrock, and Nicole Landowski. 2014. "Linking pre-meeting communication to meeting effectiveness." *Journal of Managerial Psychology* 29 (8): 1064–1081.

Allen, Joseph A., Nale Lehmann-Willenbrock, and Steven G Rogelberg. 2018. "Let's get this meeting started: Meeting lateness and actual meeting outcomes." *Journal of Organizational Behavior* 39 (8): 1008–1021.

Allison, Brooke B., Marissa L Shuffler, and Allison M Wallace. 2015. "The successful facilitation of virtual team meetings." In Joseph A. Allen, Nate Lehmann-Willenbrock, and Steven G Rogelberg (eds.), *Cambridge Handbook of Meeting Science*, 680–705. Cambridge University Press.

Boivie, Steven, Michael Bednar, Ruth Aguilera, and Joel Andrus. 2016. "Are boards designed to fail? The implausibility of effective board monitoring." *Academy of Management Annals* 10: 319–407. doi: 10.5465/19416520.2016.1120957.

Cohen, Melissa, Steven Rogelberg, Joseph Allen, and Alexandra Luong. 2011. "Meeting design characteristics and attendee perceptions of staff/team meeting quality." *Group Dynamics: Theory, Research, and Practice* 15: 90–104. doi: 10.1037/a0021549.

Kauffeld, Simone, and Nale Lehmann-Willenbrock. 2012. "Meetings matter: Effects of team meetings on team and organizational success." *Small Group Research* 43 (2): 130–158.

Keith, Elise. 2015. 55 million: A fresh look at the number, effectiveness, and cost of meetings in the U.S. *Lucid Meetings Blog.* https://blog.lucidmeetings.com/blog/fresh-look-number-effectiveness-cost-meetings-in-us.

Leach, Desmond J., Steven G Rogelberg, Peter B Warr, and Jennifer L Burnfield. 2009. "Perceived meeting effectiveness: The role of design characteristics." *Journal of Business and Psychology* 24 (1): 65–76.

Lehmann-Willenbrock, Nale, Joseph Allen, and Dain Belyeu. 2016. "Our love/hate relationship with meetings: Relating good and bad meeting behaviors to meeting outcomes, engagement, and exhaustion." *Management Research Review* 39: 1293–1312. doi: 10.1108/MRR-08-2015-0195.

Odermatt, Isabelle, Cornelius J König, Martin Kleinmann, Maria Bachmann, Heiko Röder, and Patricia Schmitz. 2018. "Incivility in meetings: Predictors and outcomes." *Journal of Business and Psychology* 33 (2): 263–282.

Rogelberg, S. G., D. J. Leach, P. B. Warr, and J. L. Burnfield. 2006. "'Not another meeting!'" Are meeting time demands related to employee well-being?" *Journal of Applied Psychology* 91 (1): 83–96. doi: 10.1037/0021-9010.91.1.83.

Rogelberg, Steven G, Cliff Scott, and John Kello. 2007. "The science and fiction of meetings." *MIT Sloan Management Review* 48 (2): 18–21.

Rogelberg, Steven G., Clifton W. Scott, Brett Agypt, Jason Williams, John E. Kello, Tracy McCausland, and Jessie L. Olien. 2014. "Lateness to meetings: Examination of an unexplored temporal phenomenon." *European Journal of Work and Organizational Psychology* 23 (3): 323–341. doi: 10.1080/1359432X.2012.745988.

Yoerger, Michael, John Crowe, Joseph A Allen, and Johanna Jones. 2017. "Meeting madness: Counterproductive meeting behaviours and personality traits." *International Journal of Management Practice* 10 (3): 203–223.

Yoerger, Michael, John Crowe, and Joseph A. Allen. 2015. "Participate or else!: The effect of participation in decision-making in meetings on employee engagement." *Consulting Psychology Journal: Practice and Research* 67 (1): 65–80. doi:10.1037/cpb0000029.

Chapter 4

New Best Practices for Meetings as a Result of COVID-19

The Meeting Scientist Perspective

I n a recent open-ended survey of working adults in the United States, Joe asked, "If you were working from home due to COVID-19, think of the last virtual meeting you had and list all the challenges (if any) that emerged due to conducting the meeting online." Take a look at the answers from a random sampling of ten people participating in the survey.

Respondent #1: "Connection errors."

Respondent #2: "Connection issues."

Respondent #3: "Getting connected to the conference line."

Respondent #4: "Getting connected was a challenge."

Respondent #5: "Network was bad for some participants."

Respondent #6: "Bad network."

Respondent #7: "Server issue."

Respondent #8: "Wi-Fi problems."

Respondent #9: "My Wi-fi cutting out so my colleagues could not hear me!"

Respondent #10: "Lag, the spinning circle of death, kill me now!"

Do any of these complaints sound familiar? Joe's research identified what more than 35% of folks found challenging – getting connected and dealing with Internet-related connectivity issues. Even under the best of circumstances, it is not uncommon for one or more participants to struggle with getting connected. Sometimes this is a result of their Internet service issues, while other times it's due to Mother Nature, uncontrollable issues such as windstorms, fires, hurricanes, and so on. If anything, 2020 taught us that anything is possible in terms of challenges to how we work.

The next major category of concerns expressed by respondents about their most recent virtual meeting was technology issues. They ran the gamut of accessing files, audio issues, lack of training/knowledge about the software, screen sharing problems, and webcam issues. Essentially, all the things that make virtual meetings particularly difficult to accomplish effectively. With this in mind, we want to share some solutions within the context of meetings shaped by COVID-19.

In this chapter, we will explore:

- How are virtual meetings different now than before?
- What are the *new* best practices that account for the shift in meeting technology?
- How does this fit with the *old* best practices?
- Why making our meetings better is really just a checklist and a few tweaks away.

Beyond the Shift from Face-to-Face to Video

As discussed in the opening chapter, the pandemic shifted most meetings from face-to-face to virtual, with video becoming the dominant meeting type. However, that is certainly not the only thing that changed. Some of the data collected by Joe suggests several other things changed for all types of meetings that are worth reviewing here.

The Length of Meetings

First, the length of our meetings got shorter. Really, it's true. Take a look at the table below.

MEETING LENGTH

Format Style	October 2019	May 2020
Face-to-Face	54 min	39 min
Telephone	47 min	44 min
Video	54 min	50 min
Hybrid	63 min	49 min

As the table shows, *all* types of meetings were shortened, with the most striking perhaps being the drop from 63 minutes per meeting for hybrid meetings in October 2019, as well as the stunningly short 39 minutes for a face-to-face meeting in May 2020. These reductions in length likely mean that much of the same work of the meeting was simply taking less time to accomplish.

When Joe first showed these results to an audience of law professionals, one astute observer said, "Well, isn't this just because the default for Zoom is 40 minutes for the free version?" If that were the case, video meetings would've dropped to around 40 minutes, but that would likely have not impacted the rest. We can speculate that perhaps the shorter face-to-face meetings are a function of a lack of desire to sweat under a mask and struggle to hear folks in the meeting. However, again, the reduction in time is not simply a function of mask-wearing or video conference software. We'll discuss this in more detail later, but the kicker is that meetings are generally just as effective now as before.

The Number of People in a Meeting

Second, another surprising finding is that meetings, for the most part, got smaller, with fewer people asked to be in attendance.

MEETING SIZE

Format Style	October 2019	May 2020
Face-to-Face	16 people	10 people
Telephone	18 people	10 people
Video	19 people	11 people
Hybrid	19 people	22 people

That's right, as the table indicates, in all cases except for hybrid meetings, our meetings got smaller. Fewer attendees across the board mean fewer pizzas for the face-to-face meeting, fewer people talking over each other (or completely ignoring each other) in the teleconference, fewer people comprising the moving photo gallery on the video conference, and frankly, fewer expenses related to meetings in general.

One thing that Joe likes to remind organizations is that meetings are expensive. They are one of the most expensive things that we do in organizations. More is spent on meetings in terms of salary, meeting spaces, and just time in general than on pretty much everything else that is done in many organizations, particularly knowledge-based organizations. After all, the cost of a meeting is not difficult to compute, with one caveat. Take the salaries of all the folks in the room/virtual space, figure out their hourly rate, and then add it up for the length of the meeting. The caveat is the opportunity cost because they could likely do other work if they were not stuck in a meeting.

Perhaps it should come as no surprise that organizations are finding that in some cases, they are just as productive or even more productive in the new virtual work-from-home situation. If the meeting size finding shared here holds true in most organizations, that means people may actually be spending a bit less time in meetings *and* spending more time doing something else, like working on other important tasks for the organization.

Why We Meet

A third important shift that occurred pertained to the reasons that we meet. We know that meetings are rather flexible in terms of purpose. We use them for decision-making, strategic planning, project updates, general reporting, and budget meetings—just to name a few. Before COVID-19, many of our meetings included training, planning, decision-making, and other collaborative processes. Since then, the data suggests that people are spending more time on information sharing and routine meetings. This is relatively easily explained by our current situation. More information-sharing meetings are needed because we can't just pop into Suzanne's office and get a quick question answered. We don't bump into Bob at the water cooler. With dispersed teams, we can't gather information as easily, so we need information and routine meetings to fill in the gaps. But why have planning and training meetings been put on the back burner? Well, in May 2020 when this data was collected, no one knew what was to come in the next day, let alone the next year. Planning for the future and the training that helps with that future probably took a back seat given all of the ambiguity in the world. We simply do not know the future or cannot predict it as reliably as pre–COVID-19, so those sorts of meetings were less prevalent.

What Tools We Use for Meetings

We also observed a fourth shift – one not based on the data presented here but no less verifiable – the quick adoption of headsets, external webcams, high-efficiency audio equipment, a second (or in Joe's case, third) screen, and so on. There was a major run on technology equipment that matched the aforementioned increase in the use of videoconferencing software. As late as August 2020, Logitech, the world's #1 provider of webcams, had a major shortage and were doing "everything they can" to diversify suppliers, adjust supply chain networks, and get the raw materials to the manufacturers to answer the call for these tools (Ehrhardt 2020).

Although the shortage occurred, the demand remained. Many quickly realized their built-in webcam on their laptop was fine for a call here and there, but not for eight hours of video conference meetings. For folks with darker home offices, an external webcam allowed for a much sharper image because it can make do with less lighting. Grainy images be gone! With those who were also sharing their spaces with kids doing online school, or other equally distracting companions (i.e. partners, cats, dogs, etc.), noise-canceling headphones that could link in and provide uninterrupted audio were a hot commodity. As will be made clear later, high-quality video and audio are a new best practice for effective virtual meetings.

Amidst the Shift, *New* Best Practices Emerged

Based upon the findings just shared and the growing body of evidence from researchers, organizations, and news sources, new best practices have emerged to help optimize the workplace meeting in a virtual environment. This section introduces some of the main new best practices based on Joe's work as a meeting scientist. However, many more best practices exist for on-camera communication, which is the subject of Chapters 5 and 6. These best practices concern virtual meetings in general.

Turn on the Camera

The first new best practice for virtual meetings is rather simple: turn on the camera. It is tempting to either use the telephone or simply turn off the camera in our meetings. This "turn off" behavior may be for a variety of reasons, as we will discuss in Chapter 5, but it remains problematic regardless. The camera is the great equalizer in virtual meetings. It requires our attention. As soon as it is off, distractions are amplified and multitasking becomes all too easy. Evidence suggests that multitasking in meetings is one of the most counterproductive meeting behaviors that hampers meeting effectiveness, as mentioned in Chapter 3. When the camera is on, it's hard to divide our attention without others noticing. In fact, Joe has seen people explain why they are looking away from the camera when on virtual calls where video is required (e.g. "I'm not ignoring you, just looking at the agenda on my other screen here" or similar statements). This at least demonstrates an acknowledgment of how it must look to their fellow attendees and is actually a best practice when body language might send out the wrong signals.

In addition to helping maintain attention, keeping the camera on helps us avoid being distracted by other things in our environment and notifies others in the room that we are occupied. In fact, just today, Joe was on a call with a colleague without video on when his partner walked into his office. When she realized she would not be caught on camera, she felt it appropriate to grab a book or two off the shelf beside him and shuffle through some papers. While her actions weren't distracting to the person Joe was meeting with, it was certainly distracting to Joe to have someone else in close orbit. Now, had the camera light been on and his partner been able to sneak a peek at the many talking heads in the video conference, she would have waited and come back later. Based on the qualitative data collected in May, Joe's not the only one who has distractions from his partner, kids, pets, and so forth. But, with the exception of the pets (and perhaps some of your kids), most others will avoid causing distraction when they could be caught on camera.

The camera also allows for context cues and nonverbal communication. As already mentioned, humans absolutely rely on nonverbal communication to help convey the meaning of their message. Sarcasm often falls flat on a teleconference, particularly when people do not know each other well. But, on a video call, one can roll their eyes, put their hands up and to the side, and sigh, thereby clarifying the intention for folks unfamiliar with their brand of humor. This is just one of the thousands of examples of nonverbal clues that we employ when interacting with other humans that are only possible when we see them, even if only through the lens of a camera. The camera is a richer medium through which to communicate, so lost in translation experiences are minimized.

Leverage the Right Technology Tools

"You're on mute." If each of us had a nickel for every time we heard or even said those words, we would have amassed a tidy sum in our bank accounts. However, the converse practice of not muting when you should is just as problematic and brings us to the second new best practice – use of the available technology.

Most video conference software has tools such as mute for audio. When you are not talking, muting can help eliminate background noise that may not be apparent to you but is very apparent to your fellow meeting attendees. If you are a meeting organizer, you often have the power to mute others, though you may be hesitant to use it. The advice here and from most communication scholars is to use the technology, figure out new norms for your team, and allow the tools to assist in collaborative efforts.

Another tool at your fingertips on most videoconferencing platforms is a chat function. For small groups (i.e. three to five participants in a meeting) chat is not typically necessary. But as the group gets larger, chat may be a way to share information with specific individuals or with the whole group without interrupting a presenter or the speaker. It provides another channel for communication that can enhance the meeting. However, it can be misused, so even as we recommend using it for larger groups, take care not to get distracted by the very thing that could be beneficial when used properly.

Many video conference tools also allow for sharing the screen, a function most are familiar with, but use only to share slides as part of a presentation. The real benefit of sharing the screen is recognizing that you're not in a large conference room doing a presentation, but you're in everyone's little office (or kitchen table) where they can see with perfect clarity on their own screen. Thus, sharing documents of all types is possible and highly useful in many cases. It's no longer necessary to somehow get the report to fit into a slide deck. One can actually show the report itself, talk through the executive summary, and show the meaningful graphics that were tirelessly prepared and would otherwise never even be seen. In other words, allow the technology to serve you, rather than try to fit old habits into the new situation.

Be Social

A third new best practice is to build in time for social interaction. Many are experiencing a sudden lack of social interaction with colleagues. For some, that's a true blessing and we understand your plight. However, for others, this lack of informal interaction sacrifices the chance to ask informal questions, discuss ideas for the future, or even stumble into some moments of brilliance over a pint (hopefully not a literal stumble, however potentially entertaining for colleagues). In all seriousness, lack of social interaction creates feelings of isolation, from both a work accomplishment and a human connection perspective, as many folks derive meaning from their relationships at work.

To combat this, embrace the idea of scheduling a little extra social interaction time. This can happen in a variety of ways. When you know a meeting has a light agenda, maybe build in a few minutes for casual talk. Ask people how they're doing. Discuss the weather, the latest antics of people's kids, or the last book people read (or television show they binge-watched). At the same time, recognize that the camera may often provide a window into your colleague's world. Allow that window to create empathy, understanding, and a sense of togetherness. Ask about the books in their background or the plant they appear to be killing. Research confirms that small talk in the form of pre-meeting chat can foster effective meetings, and that finding still applies now, perhaps more so (Yoerger, Allen, and Crowe 2018).

Safety First

Our fourth new best practice is to embrace the distance as a protection to you and your colleagues. Perhaps the obvious protection it affords is from the sharing of germs, including potential COVID-19. And yes, there is huge value in that; we are blessed to be able to still gather remotely and see each other regularly. Yet, there are other protections.

Preliminary findings in Joe's research indicates that videoconferencing also protects against unequal sharing. The data suggests that participation is more equal on video conference than was previously experienced in face-to-face meetings. There's no back of a room during a video meeting. Everyone's box is the same size on the screen, and as long as video is on, there's no hiding in the corner. And unlike face-to-face meetings, where side conversations, whispers, and other behaviors are common, everyone must address the entire meeting in video. As a meeting scientist, Joe's curious about what the capability of whispering to one person in the room might do to the effectiveness of the meeting, but he recognizes that for this reason, videoconferencing can allow for more egalitarian turn-taking. If someone is to participate, either they have to forcefully chime in *or* the meeting leader has to provide opportunity by calling on people by name. While this can require more of the facilitator to seek input from everyone on the screen, it can result in more equal sharing and more egalitarian turn-taking. We will touch on best practices for meeting moderators in Chapter 8.

Old Best Practices Still Hold True

If you just read Chapter 3, you'll notice some parallels between the new best practices and some of the old best practices. That's because most of the old best practices are still relevant in the virtual meeting. Before the meeting, identifying goals, preparing an agenda, right-sizing the meeting, and so on still apply. Finding the right meeting space is now using the right meeting software.

Best practices for during the meeting, such as participating in the meeting, avoiding complaining, using procedural communication, following the prepared agenda, and so forth, all still apply. You even have some new tools like the omnipotent mute button to shut down Bill's monologues or to remind folks that we do not need to complain about that same problem again that we all know is *not going away!* Thus, the new best practice technology tools may help facilitate the old best practice behaviors.

After the meeting, minutes should still be shared, action items should be noted, and accountability should be checked both in terms of the action items and in terms of the meeting effectiveness/satisfaction. In fact, there are some emerging tools that may allow for immediate feedback that we'll discuss further in later chapters.

Thus, the intuitive nature of meeting science and effective meeting management carries forward into our changed working environment. We still recommend the checklists shared in Chapter 3, but here's another one for virtual meetings that absorbs the new best practices and can be an additional supplement to the previous checklist. Given that you likely had a virtual meeting recently, complete this new checklist and put it together with your previous last meeting checklist. Consider how things are looking for you in terms of optimizing your meetings.

Checklist of Best Practices from the Last Virtual Meeting

Best Practices for Virtual Meetings	Yes or No
1. Are all attendees' cameras on?	[ ] Yes [ ] No
2. Are technology features used appropriately (e.g., mute all)?	[ ] Yes [ ] No
3. Are chat features used appropriately?	[ ] Yes [ ] No
4. Are screen sharing features used appropriately?	[ ] Yes [ ] No
5. Is time built in for socialization?	[ ] Yes [ ] No
6. Are all attendees encouraged to participate equally?	[ ] Yes [ ] No
7. Is the meeting software functioning?	[ ] Yes [ ] No
8. Can all attendees access the virtual meeting space?	[ ] Yes [ ] No
TOTAL YES	

Conclusion

Now, with your reflections from Chapter 3 in hand, and this new checklist completed for your recent virtual meeting, consider how many counterproductive meeting behaviors you saw, how many "old" best practices were present, and how many "new" best practices were followed. It is likely you have some successes and some areas for tweaking. We do not recommend trying to change everything at once, but set a goal that allows you to make steady progress. However, if you are going to prioritize one of the new best practices, turning the camera on would be a good choice. In the next section, we will turn our attention to video communication and how to personally optimize your on-camera experiences while improving the meeting experiences for those around you.

Chapter Takeaways

- All meetings are shorter and smaller than they were before COVID-19, which has implications for how we meet.

- Meeting types have shifted to being more about sharing information than about planning due to changes in the work and world environment.

- New best practices for the virtual meeting include turning on the camera, using the technology to help, building in time for social interaction, and embracing the distance as protection.

- *Most* of the old best practices still apply, including all the before, during, and after intuitive meeting behaviors.

- Self-reflection on our virtual meetings, using the three checklists included in this section, may provide key insights worth keeping in mind.

References

Ehrhardt, Michelle. 2020. "Logitech on webcam shortage: 'We're doing everything we can.'" *Tom's Hardware*. https://www.tomshardware.com/news/logitech-webcam-shortage-update.

Yoerger, Michael, Joseph A. Allen, and John Crowe. 2018. "The impact of premeeting talk on group performance." *Small Group Research* 49 (2): 226–258.

PART THREE

The Benefits and Challenges
of Video Communication

I t would be fair to say that very few people were pining for the days when video would become the primary way people would communicate for work. Those who love seeing themselves on camera are in a definite minority. However, the pandemic cast almost all knowledge workers into the role of on-camera communicator.

Even before the events of 2020, though, video was spreading across the corporate landscape in many forms. Why? You would be hard-pressed to find a more powerful medium that knows no geographic boundaries. For businesses with global teams, video was already becoming an important tool for internal communication, often in the form of asynchronous video. Think of enterprise-wide messages delivered on camera by the CEO and then sent out via email or the company intranet. But as the usage increased and the video production tools became more accessible, little attention was paid to empowering those who would be communicating through it. It was assumed that speaking to a camera was just like speaking to someone in person. As many people will attest, this assumption is patently untrue.

In this section, Karin raises our awareness about the potential threats of poor on-camera performance within the context of a world more reliant on video communication than ever. She highlights some barriers to effective virtual video communication and how to deal with the inevitable distractions (Chapter 5). She then shifts the focus to best practices for speaking via video, combining theory with practical application tips you can implement immediately (Chapter 6).

The Value of Video in the Corporate World

The On-Camera Coach Perspective

I n the mid-2000s, Karin left her job as a TV news anchor and reporter to apply her skills in the corporate world, and there was plenty of opportunity. With a wealth of media channels to fill and more coming on board almost daily, businesses leapt to fill those channels with their own video content. Often, that meant hiring people like Karin to be professional on-camera spokespeople, but over a period of a few years, she recognized a trend. More and more of her spokesperson gigs involved performing on camera alongside company employees pulled from the corner office or even the corner cubicle.

This propensity to use "real people" for corporate videos exposed a significant skills gap. It was assumed that if someone was an eloquent and compelling speaker to an audience in the same room, he or she would be equally captivating on camera. Unfortunately, this misperception was often exposed at the worst possible time – mid-production. No matter how many suggestions the producer or the director made, the performance level of the on-camera neophyte typically continued to tank, leaving the production staff shaking their heads and the C-level executive shaking in his shoes, having recognized his or her contribution to the video was subpar.

Speaking on camera requires a totally different skill set than delivering a message to a live audience in person. The most confident public speakers can be reduced to a puddle of sweat as soon as they realize "they're on." And these videos are usually fairly high stakes, with a significant investment of time, energy, and money. Imagine how frustrating it must be when weeks of planning and preparation are all for naught once a "star" steps in front of the camera and fails miserably.

At the outset, this was the skill gap Karin's training firm endeavored to fill – on-camera communication coaching for senior leaders or de facto spokespeople who never imagined they would be asked or even required to speak via video.

Nearly a decade later, the need for on-camera communication skills is no longer reserved for a select few. In fact, the demand for these skills exploded as COVID-19 hit and *everyone* went to virtual communication as their primary or only form of communication. Indeed, entire enterprises are trying to level up their collective skillset to best navigate a world where video is the primary channel through which they are communicating.

In this chapter, we will explore:

- What is at risk if video communication skills are not properly honed.
- Why speaking on a webcam is so different from speaking face-to-face.
- How distractions on camera threaten to derail us.
- How to handle inevitable interruptions in video meetings.

The Risks of Poor On-Camera Awareness in Video Meetings

When the pandemic took hold, nearly every in-person interaction became a virtual one. While few people were thrilled with the change, there were certainly some who managed the transition with aplomb. You can probably identify them within your organization. They're the ones who not only were early adopters of "webcam on" but when they did start their video, they looked like they had a professional set designer, had studio-level lighting, and just naturally knew what camera angle worked best.

For every example of "what good looks like," though, there are dozens, if not hundreds, of examples of webcam whiffs. The problem is that the importance of all of these meetings has not diminished, but without a full understanding of how to communicate effectively on the virtual video platform, the outcomes of those meetings are at risk.

Think about the "all-hands meeting" that became an enterprise-wide video event. Sure, a whole team likely spent weeks choosing the right tool and selecting people to support the senior executives who would be speaking. All well and good. But what they did not account for was a total lack of awareness on the part of said executives about the need to speak into the webcam or even to take a look at what his or her "shot" looked like before going live. The result? An hour-long meeting with awkward handoffs between members of the leadership team who were seen in profile or looking down . . . or who were only visible in silhouette because they had chosen to sit in front of a window. This "all-hands meeting" was intended to calm ragged nerves of employees who were dealing with the uncertainties of the times. Due to the lack of on-camera awareness, the message fell flat.

The swing-and-miss examples are many – virtual sales calls that led nowhere, internal training that didn't result in behavioral change, and team cohesion that started to fray as the wear-and-tear of dispersion took a real toll. When video is done poorly, it not only fails to be a suitable replacement to face-to-face meetings, but it becomes a window into the shared chaos of our new virtual meeting lives.

But it doesn't have to be this way. Those who figure out how to harness the power of videoconferencing will win in the age of COVID-19 and beyond. It begins with understanding why video communication requires a different approach and then adjusting accordingly. Many organizations are doing just that, but there are those who still refuse to adapt and do so at their own peril. Those who lag behind in leveraging video in their meetings internally and externally may find themselves falling farther behind their competitors who pivoted more quickly and embraced it.

Why Is Speaking to a Camera So Much Harder Than Speaking to a Person?

If you want to make someone freeze up, pull out a video camera. Its mere presence immediately changes the temperature in the room and makes most people feel suddenly uncomfortable in their own skin. This unfortunate consequence has a direct impact on our ability to communicate well via video because the best on-camera communicators have figured out how to be their absolute, genuine, authentic selves when speaking to a lens.

The barriers to our authenticity on camera are many, but we have compiled our top three that most people encounter. Perhaps you can find solace in knowing that you are not alone in feeling challenged by these obstacles, which the vast majority of us confront any time we are in a virtual video engagement.

Barrier #1: The Camera Offers No Feedback

When we talk to someone in person, we are typically taking constant inventory of their body language. Maybe that person is nodding along in agreement with what we are saying. Maybe our conversation partner is looking distracted and disinterested in what you are conveying. Whatever signals those nonverbals are sending, we react to them by adjusting our delivery. We backtrack on content we just covered because someone is looking confused or infuse even more energy into our verbal delivery to try to corral attention in another, more compelling way.

When videoconferencing, even if we are able to sneak a peek at the small box occupied by our conversation partner on the screen, we have far fewer data points to fully ascertain how our message is being greeted. In fact, as you will learn in the next chapter, if you are following best practices, you will primarily be looking at the camera when you are speaking anyway. However, this creates a void of understanding that cannot be easily overcome. Video gives us limited clues to figure out how people are reacting to what we are saying. That incomplete picture can be frustrating as a communicator and lessen our effectiveness as speakers.

In addition, we also lack those social cues that we feed off of when we speak to someone face-to-face, resulting in a flattening of our affect (Walther, Loh, and Granka 2005). Often our facial expressions and other nonverbals reflect those of our conversation partner. Think about when you take a picture of someone, and in an attempt to elicit a smile, you exclaim, "Say *Cheese*." Chances are you are grinning away yourself, mirroring what the subject of your photo is doing.

The camera doesn't give you anything to play off of, and consequently we tend to lose our typical emotiveness and animation. It's like the lens sucks all of the energy out of our delivery and makes us appear disconnected. We might be saying the right words, but our

73

body language doesn't reflect the meaning behind them. You likely have seen this happen to colleagues. Someone who is normally very animated in person suddenly becomes wooden – and dare we say "boring" – when speaking on camera. Why? Well, the source of his energy has been stolen from him. He likely feeds off the reactions of his audience, and if he can't easily read those responses, he loses a large part of his authenticity.

Barrier #2: We Are Hyper-Aware of Our Physical Selves

When we started using virtual video tools, we encountered something that we likely never saw before: a chance to watch ourselves communicate and present in real time. Our visage was both distracting and disconcerting for many of us. Who *was* that person on the screen?

Remember when you first heard your voice on your voicemail message or even your answering machine? What was your initial thought? You may have said to yourself, "I don't sound like *that*." Well, the bottom line is that you probably do to some degree, but the way you hear yourself is different than the way others hear you. The sound of our own voices can feel grating to our own ears, even when it's not to others.

The same holds true for watching ourselves present on camera. The vast majority of people cringe when having to watch themselves communicating on video. Even those who have been doing it for decades (like Karin) don't enjoy the experience. Sure, you might get more comfortable with it over time, but that feeling of "ugh" rarely goes away entirely. To make matters worse, we see things that no one else sees, and usually we pick out things that we don't like while disregarding the positive.

Allow this case in point. For every on-camera communication class, Karin has her clients do a baseline performance and a post-training performance, so they can see how they've grown throughout the process. One particular learner had come a long way, something that was confirmed when the entire class, including that presenter, watched her second video together.

When the video drew to a captivating close, Karin was grinning ear to ear and turned her attention to what she considered her star pupil of that session. What she saw puzzled her. Instead of a shining look of satisfaction, she saw a crinkled forehead and a look of almost disdain. Confused, she ventured a question, "So . . . what did you think?" The star pupil's response: "My right eyebrow is higher than my left eyebrow."

Karin couldn't help but laugh because she honestly had not noticed anything of the sort. In fact, the entire class piled on the praise for what truly had been a fabulous performance, hoping to banish any obsession about eyebrow "misplacement" from that student's mind.

However, this illustrates what we all must combat. We are our own worst critics of both real and imaginary flaws.

Barrier #3: It Feels Like a Performance

Bringing a camera into the equation has a way of unfairly elevating any communication via video to the level of a performance that makes it feel so much more high stakes. And what do we want to do when we perform? We want to be perfect. And the harder we try to be perfect, the more arduous and impossible that task becomes.

That quest for perfection strips away layers of authenticity that are tough to reclaim. We are so focused on being on our best behavior in every possible way that we lose our ability to be ourselves. The result is a contrived version of ourselves that comes across as fake – a lack of authenticity magnified by the camera lens.

If you look at all three of these barriers, you might recognize a single source: you. The biggest barrier to your authenticity is your inability to get outside of your head. When we are in a virtual video environment, often we are engaging in a world that we are simultaneously a part of and not a part of. Our physical selves are in a separate room, a separate state, and possibly even a separate country than where we are supposed to be mentally, and the chasm that it creates leaves plenty of room for distractions to derail us.

Distraction Danger

When speaking on a webcam, your audience or your conversation partner can only see a small slice of what is going on in your environment, but what can be seen within that window may be the only calm in what you know is total chaos. Just out of frame, there may be a multitude of housekeeping sins hidden from view, children waiting not so patiently for their lunch to be prepared, or a partner who is trying to conduct her own business call while you carry on with yours. However, while your audience might not have the 360° view, you certainly do, and the threat of distractions is ever-present.

Your carefully curated background might not belie the fact that you have a cat jumping from the couch to the chair just a few feet from your laptop. What about your twelve-year-old who needs your help right *now* on an algebra problem and busts into the room despite the note on the door saying, "Please don't interrupt. I'm on a call." Better yet, how about the family dog who had been sleeping peacefully but then awoke to gag on the Kleenex he consumed from the trash – a last-ditch effort to get your attention once and for all. All of this could be going on while you are in the midst of an important presentation for one of your premiere clients, and your job is to act as if all is copacetic in your world.

Managing all of these distractions creates an extra cognitive burden that can impact how well we communicate in the moment and can even lead to us suffering "brain cramps" where you forget something you can't imagine ever forgetting. It's no wonder popular press started talking about "Zoom fatigue" and "Webex weariness," as we tried to hide the many work-from-home distractions occurring around our video conferences.

During virtual meetings, you can only control what is controllable. You know that you should never do meetings at 10 a.m. in the room at the front of your house because your neighbor always blows leaves off the sidewalk at that time every day. But there can be and usually will be interruptions that you simply can't plan for or avoid. When they happen, you have to do a quick assessment of the situation. Does my audience know that something is amiss? Should I keep plowing ahead as if nothing is going on? Should I stop what I am doing to address it?

Suffice it to say, the ever-present threat of distractions creates a very real danger to our ability to communicate well on camera.

An Early "Kid Cameo"

In 2017, a family blooper went viral in a way that would barely register as a blip in today's work-from-home culture. Robert Kelly is better known as "BBC Dad." At the time of his rise to fame, he was an associate professor of political science at Pusan National University in South Korea who was speaking live from his home office with the BBC's James Menendez about the ouster of South Korean President Park Geun-hye (Stump 2020).

In the middle of giving his insights, his daughter, Marion, a comically dramatic 4-year-old, dances into the room behind him in full view for the audience (BBC News 2017). The interviewer identified the proverbial elephant in the room ("I think one of your children has just walked in"), tipping Kelly off to the fact that his online interview sanctum had been breached. Not to be outdone, seconds later his 9-month-old son, James, rolled into the picture in one of those walkers on wheels. But perhaps the most relatable character appeared only a moment later, his wife, Kim Jung-A, who bounded into the room looking mortified but determined to remove them all from the remote BBC set.

Kelly offered a few apologies as well as a quick chuckle but didn't even glance behind him to survey the scene. He did perform a quick arm sweep to keep Marion from creeping even closer to the camera, but for the most part, he appeared nonplussed aside from a prolonged closing of his eyes, a nonverbal version of "serenity now." Kelly kept answering the questions he was asked and continued to expound upon the political shifting sands in the region.

How to Deal with the Interruptions

Let's put that moment into the context of 2020 post-February. By now, everyone has experienced the kid cameo, the cat cameo, and myriad other interruptions that punctuate our virtual meetings. Today, Kelly might have picked young Marion up and placed her on his lap while continuing to speak eloquently on the topic at hand, or if he knew that his hilarious daughter wouldn't be satisfied with sitting quietly, maybe he would have asked his interviewer for a quick break to escort his children out of the room and off camera.

You too may have to make quick decisions on how to deal with your own version of the Kelly kid cameo. In 2017, Kelly chose to deal with the situation by mostly ignoring it, which raised some eyebrows and spawned some interesting theories. After he was repeatedly asked why he didn't stand up and escort his little ones out of the room, he wrote an article in *The Interpreter*, published by the Lowy Institute, to explain his actions. He said he worried about not looking professional, and "the show must go on" (Kelly 2018). It also allowed him to put to rest, once and for all, the rumor that he hadn't been wearing any pants.

So, what can we learn from this early example of meeting interruptions?

Don't pretend it's not happening. If your audience can see it or hear it, you can't wish that away. The issue with Kelly's approach was that it rang false to every person who viewed the clip. Anyone who was watching it *knew* it was happening, and not acknowledging it seemed a bit out of place.

At the time, the incident spurred thousands of work-from-home employees to reach out to Kelly and his family, expressing their support for what they could so easily relate to. "These reactions were positive and empathetic," according to Kelly. Had he known the empathy he generated, he likely would have handled the situation differently.

The sudden shift to remote work has also afforded a much higher level of grace being given to coworkers who may be in work-from-home situations with many inherent challenges. Early advice to those who found themselves in makeshift home offices was to give their teammates a tour of their spaces. Let them see that you are sharing your small apartment with three people who are all doing Zoom calls a few feet from each other. Feature your four dogs, two cats, and your chatty parrot on your Teams meeting so your coworkers recognize that your best may not be good enough to keep the entire menagerie quiet at all times. Understanding breeds empathy and often uncovers common ground.

Three Easy Steps

Step 1: Acknowledge it

Rather than turning a blind eye to the obvious, first admit what is happening. If you are in a meeting with those who are familiar with your work environment, you can refer to a known challenge. For example, when your dog starts barking as the UPS truck pulls up your driveway, you can make a joke that he's protecting you again from the existential threat of the delivery guy.

If you are in a meeting with someone new, acknowledge the interruption, offer a quick apology, and move on to Step 2.

Step 2: Take action

Determine the most efficient way to deal with it. The longer you fret about how embarrassing this is, the longer you take away from the business at hand. Make a quick decision on how you can address it swiftly.

Say your 12-year-old barges in and asks for help with a homework problem; you can simply say "excuse me a second" to your conversation partner, turn to your son, and explain succinctly that you are unable to help until after your meeting. If that preteen continues to press, then you might want to exercise the next option. Tell your conversation partner you will be right back. Turn off your video, mute your audio, and more sternly impress upon your child that you will not help him until you are finished with your work call before escorting him out.

Step 3: Get back to business

Once it has been addressed, proceed with the meeting without looking back. Resist the urge to over-apologize. It just prolongs the awkwardness. The sooner you move on, the sooner your conversation partner will, too.

Interruptions happen. The only thing you can have total control over is how you handle them. The specific approach you take will change based upon what form those interruptions take, but the key is to be decisive and efficient in addressing them so as to waste as little mind space and meeting time as possible.

A Story from Karin's Perspective

It was 8:40 a.m., and I had a decision to make. Do I let my hundred-some-pound St. Bernard continue to snooze in the corner of my office or do I summarily wake him up and usher him out? My three-hour workshop was due to start in 20 minutes, and I had to open up the Zoom meeting in 5 minutes.

With both of my human children off at college, Bailey has become my only child and, like many only children, is spoiled rotten. So you might have guessed what I decided to do. My rather large pup remained in the room with me as I flicked on my ring light, clipped on my lapel microphone, and opened the call.

All went fine for a while. My participants were engaged and soaked in the content while Bailey peacefully and ever so quietly snored away. But then things changed. The snoring became a snort as she jolted awake and decided she no longer wanted to be in the room. She bolted for the door – a door that was unfortunately closed.

Oh, if only dogs had opposable thumbs!

Bailey is not a barker, but she is a moaner. In order to interpret the moans, you need to use context clues. In this case, her moans, which were growing increasingly in volume and duration, indicated she wanted out and she wanted out now.

I had a decision to make, and it had to be made fast. Do I hope that my class could not hear her and just continue to teach as if nothing was amiss, or do I model good behavior and address the elephant . . . or rather, the dog almost the size of an elephant in the room?

I opted for the latter. I asked them to excuse me for a few seconds, turned off my video and muted my audio, let Bailey take care of whatever urgent matter she needed to attend to, and then sat down in front of the lens once more. It took less than 30 seconds for me to problem-solve the interruption (albeit of my own making). I was able to beg quick forgiveness, share a laugh, and move on with *the workshop. What was most valuable, though, was for them to see me "walk the walk." I followed my own advice for dealing with interruptions.*

What I did not follow was my advice for controlling what is controllable, even when it comes in the form of an almost irresistible furry face.

Conclusion

Like it or not, video communication has found a foothold in corporate culture and will likely be a medium that is used well beyond the pandemic. Honing your on-camera skills can be a career differentiator, allowing you to stand out from the crowd, especially when so much business is getting done via virtual means. But what do you need to know to be a truly effective virtual video communicator? Find out in our next chapter.

Chapter Takeaways

- Speaking on camera requires a different skill set than speaking to an audience in the same room.

- Poor on-camera performance can lead to poor business outcomes, including unsuccessful sales calls, uninspiring internal messaging, and a loss of team cohesion.

- Authenticity is what works best for speaking via video, but there are many barriers to being our genuine selves on camera.

- The camera offers no feedback on how our message is resonating, which can flatten our affect and make us appear disconnected and disinterested.

- Virtual video meetings allow us to see ourselves communicate in real time, which can be disconcerting and distracting.

- When speaking on a camera, even a small one, it feels more like a performance than a meeting, which leads to a fruitless quest for perfection.

- Distractions beyond the view of the camera, unbeknownst to our viewers but very apparent to us, threaten to derail our ability to communicate effectively.

- Follow three steps when dealing with interruptions:
  - Acknowledge it.
  - Take action.
  - Get back to business.

References

BBC News. 2017. "Children interrupt BBC News interview - BBC News." BBC News. https://www.youtube.com/watch?v=Mh4f9AYRCZY&feature=emb_logo.

Kelly, Robert E. 2018. "A year of internet stardom: 'BBC Dad' reflects." *The Interpreter*. Lowy Institute. https://www.lowyinstitute.org/the-interpreter/year-internet-stardom--bbc-dad-reflects.

Stump, Scott. 2020. *"'BBC Dad' reflects on viral work-from-home moment: 'Mostly fun, sometimes weird.'" Today*. NBC Universal. https://www.today.com/parents/bbc-dad-revisits-his-family-s-viral-moment-one-year-t124934.

Walther, Joseph B., Tracy Loh, and Laura Granka. 2005. "Let me count the ways: The interchange of verbal and nonverbal cues in computer-mediated and face-to-face affinity." *Journal of Language and Social Psychology* 24 (1): 36–65.

Chapter 6

Best Practices for On-Camera Communication Through a Webcam

The On-Camera Coach Perspective

Decades ago, Hollywood showed us glimpses of what videoconferencing *should* be like. In 1989, you might recall that iconic scene in *Back to the Future Part II* when Marty McFly is fired by his boss who screams at him through the video monitor. To go even further back, think about that videophone that was prominently featured in *The Jetsons,* the cartoon from the 1960s that lived for decades through reruns. In both of these shows, the technology worked in a similar fashion. With a push of a button, a friend, coworker, or irate boss popped up on the screen, as ready for a conversation as if you were both in the same room. The only oddity was that you could only see the top half of the person on the screen.

Sound familiar?

Yes, the old Hollywood version of videoconferencing does resemble the real-life version today, but there's a distinct difference. In the fictionalized version, the characters could easily carry on a conversation with whoever was on screen, all while maintaining the same eye contact that they would face-to-face. Both parties could easily read each other's expressions along with hearing each other's words, all while looking straight into each other's eyes.

Unfortunately, the technology available to most of us today lacks a camera lens embedded in the screen, which limits our ability to hold natural eye contact with our conversation partners.

Imprecise eye contact is one of the many barriers to our effectiveness when speaking over a webcam, and overcoming those barriers requires a new approach, as well as a little know-how, to become as authentic as possible when communicating via video.

In this chapter, we will explore:

- The proper mental mindset when speaking on a webcam.
- Where to look during virtual meetings.
- Ways to sharpen your virtual presentation skills.
- The importance of vocal variety for comprehension of your content delivered via video.
- The use of body language appropriate to this modality.

The Mental Mindset for Speaking on a Webcam

A few years ago, Karin hosted a series of live webcasts for a tech client at their annual conference. The webcasts were conducted nearly back-to-back throughout the day, leaving no time for rehearsal. A revolving chair of interviewees came and went, with Karin mostly working through a list of questions supplied by the client. Those being interviewed displayed varying levels of comfort with appearing on camera. Some approached it simply as a conversation and acted as if the cameras weren't even there. Others were a little tenser but still managed their way through without any gaffes.

One of those webcasts was earmarked as an opportunity to interview award winners who were being celebrated at the event for their work on behalf of or in association with the company. As a university professor grabbed the stool beside her, Karin was delighted to see how relaxed and articulate she was. After a few minutes of chitchat (again, rehearsal time was in short supply), the red light went on and Karin introduced her next guest . . . and that's when things got weird.

The professor who had been so conversational and natural only a minute ago switched into what can only be described as "presenter mode." She projected her voice as if she were trying to reach the back row of a lecture hall. Her cadence became dramatically stilted. Her gestures were *big* and appeared contrived.

What happened?

The professor had misunderstood what is likely the biggest distinction between speaking to an audience in the same room and speaking on camera. When you are talking on a webcam, it's always an audience of one.

It's a Conversation

An audience of one? How can that be? Sure, sometimes you may just be videoconferencing with one person, but you have had plenty of situations where there were no fewer than 50 boxes on the screen. But while there might be 50 people on the call, when you speak, they all feel like you are talking just to them. The camera creates a conversation space for you and your audience to interact, and often that conversation space places a short distance between the two of you. It should feel less like you are standing up in front of the room and performing, and more like you are having a chat with someone across the dinner table.

Think about your last virtual meeting. No matter how many people you meet with, you are only the distance from your chair to your camera and from their camera to their eyes away. In many cases, that might be within the CDC social distance guidelines of six feet, and if you were in person you would probably feel like you are too close.

That's how it feels. Even in the gallery view of many video conference tools, the distance feels less than the geography might suggest.

Understanding that conversation zone has implications on everything you do, from how you present vocally as well as physically. You aren't going to swing your arms wildly and make big gestures to emphasize your point if you are only a few feet away from someone. No, it would feel like an invasion of their personal space. You also wouldn't feel any need to raise your voice unless they're hard of hearing – in most cases, speaking at normal volume would be appropriate when closely conversing. "Presenter mode" will appear fake to your audience, and worse, the camera will exaggerate any lack of authenticity.

Where Do I Look? The Challenge of Imprecise Eye Contact

One of the basic rules of communication is "make good eye contact with your audience." But that rule can lead you astray in a virtual video setting. If we follow that principle, you might think you should be looking at the people who are in the virtual meeting with you. Where are those people? On the screen. But what happens when you look at the screen? You actually don't appear to be making good eye contact at all. In fact, it's just the opposite. Instead, you will appear to be looking away and possibly even completely disconnected from the conversation.

TRY THIS

What you will need:

- A smartphone, webcam, or tablet that allows you to record yourself.
- A way to record yourself either natively on your device or through a video collaboration platform such as Zoom or Microsoft Teams.

Follow these steps:

1. Prepare to record yourself using the device and method of your choosing by turning on your camera and sitting within the frame.

2. Record yourself introducing yourself while looking at your image on the screen. The content is unimportant, but make sure you talk for at least 20 seconds.

3. Now, while the camera is still rolling, shift your eyes to the camera. Introduce yourself looking directly at the lens for approximately the same period of time.

4. Stop the recording and either save it to your device, or if using an online platform, allow it to convert to a video file that you can save on your device.

5. Watch your video and check out the difference between your first take when you looked at the screen and the second when you looked at the lens.

What did you notice? As the viewer, which version seemed to hold your attention better: the one where you spoke to the screen or the one where you looked at the lens? Which appeared more natural to you?

It's Not About You

No doubt, you much preferred looking at the screen, and when you are in a video meeting, you likely much prefer looking at the people who are joining you on the call. However, in order for you to be truly impactful when you speak, it is critical that you speak primarily to the lens. This will feel awkward to you, and may even go against every natural impulse that you have. You want, even *need* to look at the people you are talking to, but here's the thing . . . it's not about you.

The camera is the conduit to your conversation partner. To speak with impact, you need to direct your attention to the camera. If you engage with the lens, your viewer will feel like you are directly engaging with him or her. If you don't look at the camera, you can't connect as deeply, and you will forfeit the true power of using video as a form of communication (Bohannon et al. 2013).

Now, this does not mean you should stare at the camera lens. Of course not. You wouldn't stare at someone when speaking face-to-face, and you shouldn't when speaking via video, either. However, we sometimes overcorrect and lock our eyes on the lens. When talking to someone in person, we would sense that we are making that person feel really uncomfortable and relieve their unease by looking away. However, the camera doesn't give us that cue that we are boring a hole into our conversation partner's brain. So consider the camera as a tangible representation of a person and interact with it the way you would with someone face to face. Tricking yourself to see the camera as the person will artificially but accurately cause you to engage in appropriate interaction behavior.

Think about when you are telling a story. You may begin by looking at your rapt audience, but you are probably spending a lot of time glancing down or up or sideways as you recall parts of the narrative. You always come back to the conversation partner to ensure he or she is with you, but you don't tell that story without breaking eye contact. It would feel odd.

You may be thinking, "But I want to be able to see how they are reacting to my message. How can I do that if I'm looking at the lens?"

Remember, you do not spend 100% of your time looking at the lens when speaking. You can absolutely sneak a peek at the screen to see if people are nodding along, nodding off, or checking out. However, you want to primarily keep the focus on your audience through the camera.

However, if you are not speaking, by all means, look at the screen. That will allow you to reap the benefits of reading the body language of the person who *is* speaking. In other words, as in natural, face-to-face interaction, there is a balance to strike between eye contact and looking away as you speak. Too much eye contact is creepy, and too little eye contact suggests disinterest or distraction. It is essentially acting natural with the lens being the interaction partner and the screen being the nonverbal communication source. As you might expect, it takes practice.

Visualize Your Viewer

As mentioned in Chapter 5, when we speak to a camera, we can sometimes lose a lot of our natural expressiveness and appear less animated at best, or completely lifeless at worst. This is due in large part to the fact that we forget we actually are talking to people, not simply saying words to a piece of glass.

One of the best ways to regain your natural animation is to make a conscious effort to visualize your viewer. If you are indeed having a one-on-one video meeting, it's easy to do. When speaking to the lens, conjure up the image of the person you are conversing with in your head and allow that image to drive the genuine delivery. If you are in a meeting with multiple people, pick one person who is a representative of that audience and speak to him or her.

If this mental leap is just too much, here are a few other tricks you can try:

- Place a picture of a friend or family member right beside your camera lens as a visual reminder that you are talking to a person through the webcam.

- Put a mirror behind your webcam and talk to yourself (note that this can pose another problem, which we will address shortly).

- Put a sticky-note right beside the camera that has the words "Look at the camera" written in big enough letters to serve as a constant reminder.

Coaching yourself to do something that feels categorically unnatural takes time. You will not immediately warm to the idea, but start taking note of how others come across when they are on a call with you. Who is able to really command the virtual room: those who look at the camera when speaking, or those who do not?

Secretly, though, we are hoping the day will come soon when the Jetsons' videophone experience becomes possible for all of us.

Presenting with Slides: Guide Them with Your Gaze

If you are using a slide deck, eye contact becomes an even more vexing conundrum. Should you memorize what's on the slide and not look at your material at all? Not necessarily. It all depends upon where you want your audience to receive the information. There may be times when you want to be the source, but there may also be moments when you want them to look at the data that you are sharing on the screen. Your job is to guide them with your gaze. Let them know where they should direct their attention in two ways: look where you want them to look and then verbally cue them to reinforce it.

You may introduce a topic by looking directly into the camera in hopes of connecting through the lens, but you may then want them to take a look at the carefully crafted graph that illustrates, say, the return on investment (ROI) of the current social media campaign. At that point, you would look at the slide yourself, purposefully breaking eye contact, and then verbally cue them to also look at the slide. For example, you could say something like, "If you take a look at the graph on the slide, you can see an upward trajectory, indicating that we are gaining traction." If you want your audience to continue looking at the slide content, keep looking at the screen as well. However, if you want to deliver a key takeaway, reengage with the camera lens before saying it. That will indicate to your audience that they should be turning their attention to you. To further cement this, consider closing out the screen share so you limit their choices of where to look.

Notice that this follows best practices for presentations in a face-to-face environment, where you want them to focus on you at times and focus on the slides or visuals at other times. Why create an elaborate set of slides if you only want the attention of their eyes upon you? In a physical space, you can point. In a virtual space, depending on your software, you may or may not be able to easily point. Thus, you must use vocal cues and change in eye contact to move the audience to the correct attention location, be it you, the slides, or other visuals.

Embrace the Butterflies

Speaking on camera can be an unnerving experience. Research shows up to 85% of people fear public speaking, but even if you don't suffer that phobia, you may find your palms start to sweat when a camera is brought into the equation. That worry is actually something you can use to your advantage. Transforming that anxiety into energy will help you overcome that camera-flattening effect and the many distractions that surround you.

When Karin manned the anchor desk during her broadcast journalism career, her best newscasts were the ones devoted to breaking news. There were no scripts, little direction, and minute-by-minute changes. A plan to go live at City Hall might switch in midstream to a satellite interview with the governor. Breaking news required ultimate focus. Did those newscasts provoke anxiety? Of course! But those butterflies actually made her sharp and resulted in her being as connected and in the moment as she possibly could be. The situation demanded it.

From a scientific perspective, the sweaty palms and increased feelings of anxiety during public speaking, or on-camera with breaking news, are really a function of the fight-or-flight response (Cherry 2019). Interestingly, this response was adaptive to fighting off a predator or running from one during the presumed evolutionary past. Now, it can serve similar functions but can also potentially allow us to channel energy into focused, task-driven success, whether on camera or in other situations. The degree to which that energy can be channeled may go a long way to reacting appropriately on-camera and being a virtual meeting expert.

Therefore, when communicating via virtual video, you too can channel that nervousness into energy and focus. It will allow you to reach through the camera lens to the people with whom you are meeting and perform at a higher level than if you were lulled into complacency.

Use Your Hidden Real Estate

In Chapter 5, we talked about how easy it is to suffer a brain cramp when presenting via virtual video. Being a master of your content will lessen the likelihood of a brain cramp. However, there is another way to ward off an embarrassing moment when your mind doesn't want to recall a fact or figure. You have a wealth of hidden real estate to hide your notes and any other facilitation tools that you can leverage without your audience's knowledge.

When you present virtually, your fellow meeting participants can only see what you allow them to see through your webcam. That means you only have to keep a small sliver of your environment tidy, while chaos can be creeping at the corners of the frame. It also means you can keep your papers, index cards, extra monitor, or laptop just out of frame, all of which can hold critical information that you may need to refer to. You may feel most comfortable using multiple screens that you can toggle back and forth between, but if that requires more dexterity than you can muster, feel free to print out your notes so you can place the actual pages in a spot where they are readily accessible. Have a few numbers that you know you want to reference but are afraid you might forget? Write them down on Post-it notes and stick them to your screen. Your audience will barely notice your quick look away from the camera, but you will be aware of how much easier it is to present when you have a safety net of notes close at hand.

The Necessity of Vocal Variety in Virtual Video Presentations

Our brains are hardwired to pick up change in the environment and ignore anything that is repetitive, redundant, or expected, so imagine what can happen if you speak in a monotone or at one pace, with no pauses except for a periodic gasp for breath. When communicating via virtual video, we are constantly fighting to keep the attention of our audience. Injecting vocal variety in your delivery is one of the most effective ways to do so, and you have three main tools at your disposal: pitch, pace, and pauses.

What's Your Range?

Everyone has a different vocal range: how high your voice goes and how low your voice goes. Everyone's vocal range is unique, and one is not better than another. However, no matter how wide or narrow your range is, you need to stretch its limits. Why? Because we need to vocally highlight what is important for your audience.

If we speak at the same pitch without much variation in our inflection, our steady tone becomes white noise. Our audience will tune out. All of our laboriously prepared content will go in one ear and out the other. To combat that tendency, opt for emphasizing "meaning words" by raising your pitch. The meaning words are those that carry the gist of the message. Let's go back to those notes that you've stowed away within arm's length. Did you script out what you want to say? Did you convert them to just bullet points? Whatever format your notes are in, try underlining the meaning words. Those underlines will serve as a visual cue that will automatically remind you to emphasize them when you speak them.

TRY THIS

Let's test this out using one of the sentences you just read. Using your smartphone and whatever voice memo app you have, record yourself reading the sentence below.

The meaning words are those that carry the gist of the message.

Stop the recording, but before you play it back, let's do one more variation. We've underlined the meaning words below. Create a second recording, speaking the same sentence out loud with the visual cues inserted.

The <u>meaning</u> words are those that carry the <u>gist</u> of the message.

Now listen to the two versions of the sentence. Did you hear a difference? Perhaps you heard yourself raising your pitch or your volume a bit when you spoke the underlined words. That vocal variety will help your audience discern what is truly important for them to take in and comprehend.

First-Pass Pacing

When presenting virtually, it can almost feel like we are speaking in a vacuum, especially if you are sharing slides and don't have an array of audience members appearing on the screen with you. When we feel as if we are speaking to no one, we gain a singular focus: to get through the content as quickly as possible. To make matters worse, if we are nervous, we tend to pick up the pace. All of this can result in us delivering our presentation at warp speed.

In order for your audience to actually comprehend what you are saying, you want to seek first-pass pacing – you say it once, and your audience hears and digests it the first time through. Perhaps someone might ask you to repeat yourself, but in all likelihood, no one will. To better ensure your message sticks, you need to slow it down.

Settle into the Silence

Perhaps one of the most effective ways to command the attention of the audience on the other side of the camera is through the deft use of pauses. They are known to be effective in all types of meetings and learning how to use them may prove meaningful (Rogelberg 2018). However, while those moments of silence are critical, they can be much harder to allot when delivering virtually.

Professional video etiquette typically calls for you to be on mute when you are not speaking. It's common courtesy to not let the barking dog or the lawnmower hum creep into the auditory experience of the rest of the people on the call. However, with virtual video, the mute button also sterilizes the environment. When we meet face-to-face, there's a typical low level of background noise. It may be the sound of muffled voices from down the hall or even just the whir of the air conditioning blowing through the vents. It doesn't even register for us when we are meeting in person, but its absence is definitely felt when we are meeting remotely.

Best Practices for On-Camera Communication Through a Webcam

Any pause can feel very pregnant, especially if you are from a culture that has a low level of tolerance for silence. In fact, according to Erin Meyer, author of *The Culture Map*, people in the United States are likely to become uncomfortable with silence at the 2–2.5 second mark, at which point they typically jump in to fill that silence (Meyer 2019). While we are relieving our own discomfort, though, we are sacrificing the opportunity for our words to land with impact.

Imagine a comedian who delivers a successful punchline – but instead of giving the audience a chance to laugh, just plows right into telling another joke. What happens to the value of that punchline? It's lost or at least greatly diminished.

In order for your audience to fully appreciate what you say, you need to give your key takeaways time to land, be thoughtfully considered, and ultimately digested. But this can only happen if you give your audience time to do so. We are not suggesting a ten-second full stop. That will only feel contrived. However, a 2–3 second pause placed after delivering a key takeaway can mean the difference between making a message stick or sending it out into the ether.

Do recognize that a pause feels quite different to you as the speaker than it does to your listener. You might feel like that silence is a waste of empty space, but not so for your audience. If you have said something worth pondering, those few seconds of silence that you have created allow for what you hope is active mental engagement on the part of your listeners . . . a crucial component of speaking with impact.

How Your Body Speaks on a Webcam

Speaking on camera can sometimes feel like an out-of-body experience. Suddenly, you feel hyperaware of your physical self and have absolutely no idea what to do with your hands. But if you are thinking about what your hands are doing, you are focusing on the wrong thing. If you concentrate on the message, your body will respond organically to your content and support what you are saying.

Think about it this way. When you are talking to someone face to face in casual conversation, are you planning out your gestures? If you told your friend about your scrumptious dinner last night, you would likely not say, "I had the best steak I've ever had." (Make an "ok" sign with your right hand.) "Then, I capped it off with a slice of chocolate torte that was fantastic." (Use both hands to make a "wow" gesture.)

No, planning your gestures like that would be ridiculous. However, you would likely instinctively make appropriate gestures that supported your comments.

However, while natural gestures and body movement are preferred, there are a few nuances that you need to be aware of when speaking through that little lens.

Gestures by Frame Size

One of the biggest factors in determining what body movement works or does not work on camera is something called frame size. That's how much your audience can see of you on screen. The way you frame yourself creates the distance between you and your conversation partner, and it is key to ensure appropriate and professional spacing. If you frame yourself so all that can be seen is your head, you will come across as a "close talker." It's uncomfortable when someone invades your personal space when you are talking in person. While it's equally as uncomfortable on camera, we don't recognize our faux pas as readily. Instead of the extreme closeup, opt for one of two frame sizes: a medium shot or a tight shot.

A medium shot is where you are seen from maybe the waist up. With this framing, you are almost emulating a conversation distance of several feet – as if you are chatting with a colleague in the hall or even at a networking event. You have room to gesture, but it's more limited than if you were seen from head to toe.

A tight shot is one where you are framed from perhaps mid-chest up. This framing creates a closer conversational space, and most hand gestures that venture onto the screen will be distracting. However, do not sit on your hands. Body movement is essential even if you are off camera. We communicate not just with our words and our tone of voice but also with our whole bodies. If you try to muzzle one part of that, your overall communication effectiveness will be negatively impacted. If you hold your body stiff, your verbal delivery will be stiff and stilted as well. Allow yourself to gesture on a tight shot, but keep your gestures a bit lower so that they are off screen. If they periodically venture into frame it's not a problem. It'll make you appear more authentic.

Beware the Comfy Chair

One of the businesses that really took off during the early days of the pandemic was office furniture. Work-from-home prompted many people to purchase new desks and chairs, and many of those chairs were designed for comfort. However, if you lean back into that seat during a video meeting, you may be sending the wrong signal with your body language.

Moving away from the camera can produce a slight tilting up of your chin – a movement that is exaggerated by the lens. That chin lift can make you come across as arrogant and even a bit standoffish. Think about recreating that scenario in person. If someone backs away from you, that tends to feel like you are being slighted.

Instead, try channeling your movement toward the camera. When you lean toward the lens, that will feel very inviting to your conversation partner. Just be sure to not lean into the point where you border on "close talker" territory.

To Sit or Stand?

The lockdowns that occurred across much of the nation created a pandemic of less physical activity as well. As much as a 50% drop in physical activity was recorded in the month after stay-at-home orders were issued (DiGiulio and Millard 2020). Many Americans did not take this sitting down and bought standing desks.

Whether to sit or stand during a video meeting depends upon personal preference. If you feel like you perform best and can stay better engaged when on your feet, by all means, do so. However, make sure you don't rock back and forth in the frame, bouncing from the left side of the screen to the right. You are liable to make people seasick. To combat this, try placing one foot slightly in front of the other, which makes it almost impossible to sway side to side.

If you opt to stay seated, don't slouch. Not only does it look sloppy and unprofessional, but you also run the risk of mentally checking out. If you want to stay mentally engaged, stay more physically engaged by sitting up in your chair, not sinking back into it.

One more word of caution: beware the swivel chair. If a video meeting starts to drag on, you may find yourself yearning to move, but that wiggle from side to side is pronounced on camera when the field of view is so limited. If you can lock it down, do so in order to save your audience from suffering fits of distraction.

TRY THIS

It can be overwhelming to keep track of all of the aspects of video communication that really count, so we wanted to give you a quick reference tool. Before your next virtual meeting, run down this competency checklist to refresh your memory and recalibrate your approach for this meeting modality.

Competency Checklist

Performance Considerations

Competency	Criteria	Yes or No
Gestures	Use gestures to appear natural but keep them appropriate for frame size	[ ] Yes [ ] No
Eye Contact	Primarily look at the lens when speaking but don't stare	[ ] Yes [ ] No
Vocal Range	Use entire vocal range to draw the ear to key points	[ ] Yes [ ] No
Pacing	Present content at listener-appropriate pace	[ ] Yes [ ] No
Pausing	Use pauses to increase impact of words	[ ] Yes [ ] No
Posture	Sit or stand up straight. Slouching looks unprofessional	[ ] Yes [ ] No

Approach

Competency	Criteria	Yes or No
Audience of One	Stay in the conversation zone, not presenter mode	[ ] Yes [ ] No
Energy Level	Amp up your energy to overcome the flattening effect of the camera	[ ] Yes [ ] No
Presentation Helpers	Use hidden real estate to keep important notes close but off screen	[ ] Yes [ ] No

TOTAL YES [____]

Conclusion

Speaking via video can have its challenges, but once you understand the nuances of this form of communication, you unleash opportunities that aren't available in person. Video is immediate, intimate, and powerful, with a broader reach than in-person communication could ever offer, and by and large, it's pandemic-proof.

However, there are also many potential pitfalls to video communication and how it's used during virtual meetings. In the next section, we will address some of the biggest opportunities and challenges related to virtual meetings that we have seen develop over the months of mostly remote work and share some real-world case studies from a wide range of industries.

Chapter Takeaways

- Speaking on camera should feel like you are having a conversation with someone rather than presenting to a roomful of people. It's always an audience of one, regardless of the number of people on a call. They all feel like you are talking just to them.

- In order to connect with your audience and deliver with impact, primarily look at the camera when speaking.

- Visualize your viewer to recapture authenticity that can be lost when communicating via video.

- Transform any nervousness into energy to keep you sharp and in the moment.

- Inject vocal variety into your delivery by varying your pitch, pacing, and pausing to better ensure comprehension.

- Your gestures should be organic to your content but not distracting.

- Feel free to sit or stand for a video meeting, but make sure your movement within the frame is not distracting.

References

Bohannon, Leanne S., Andrew M. Herbert, Jeff B. Pelz, and Esa M. Rantanen. 2013. "Eye contact and video-mediated communication: A review." *Displays* 34 (2): 177–185.

Cherry, Kendra. 2019. "How the fight-or-flight response works." Verywell Mind. https://www.verywellmind.com/what-is-the-fight-or-flight-response-2795194.

DiGiulio, Sarah and Elizabeth Millard. 2020. "44 top self-care tips for taking care of you during the Coronavirus pandemic." Everyday Health. https://www.everydayhealth.com/wellness/top-self-care-tips-for-being-stuck-at-home-during-the-coronavirus-pandemic/.

Meyer, Erin. 2019. "Conversational silence." Global Leadership Network. https://globalleadership.org/videos/leading-others/conversational-silence-2.

Rogelberg, Steven G. 2018. *The Surprising Science of Meetings: How You Can Lead Your Team to Peak Performance*. Oxford University Press.

PART FOUR

The Biggest Opportunities and Challenges of Virtual Meetings

E very change in the world presents unintended consequences, both good and bad. A change in safety and hazard research focused on rewarding a lack of accidents on the job taught us that a goal of zero accidents doesn't actually reduce accidents, but reduces the *reporting* of accidents. Similarly, if we start asking for feedback on meetings without ensuring that people feel psychologically safe, they won't change how they meet but will only rate the meetings that went well, creating a halo effect around the workplace practice (i.e. "nothing to see here"). And, of course, there have been some unintended and unexpected consequences to the sudden and abrupt transition to virtual meetings.

This section focuses on the biggest opportunities and challenges presented by the preponderance of virtual meetings in the workplace, and this is where Joe and Karin's respective areas of expertise converge. With virtual meetings so often incorporating video, both speak with a unified voice on what works and what does not, sharing ideas for real-world application of best practices steeped in data-based meeting science.

In this section, we look at ways to optimize the effectiveness of the virtual meetings using video (Chapter 7), how to better engage attendees during the meeting (Chapter 8), and raise awareness of professional meeting etiquette (Chapter 9).

We also look at the challenges like ignoring the importance of how we "show up" on a webcam (Chapter 10), introducing new hires to the organizational culture when onboarding is remote (Chapter 11), and equipping employees with the right tools to succeed when meetings are remote (Chapter 12). We wrap up the section with a focus on potential blind spots when using virtual communication tools across global cultures (Chapter 13). In response, we share some case studies of those who have capitalized on the opportunities while also mitigating the challenges – something only those who have embraced the meeting science *and* on-camera best practices can accomplish.

Chapter 7

Making Every Virtual Meeting a Video Meeting

The Converged Perspective

As a meeting scientist, when Joe takes part in organizational meetings, he occupies an unusual position. While his primary role might be that of a participant, he can't help but make observations that set his scientific mind in motion. Allow him to share a few recent experiences from his perspective as a virtual meeting attendee:

A Story from Joe's Perspective

Observation #1: *"The other day, I was in a virtual meeting. One of about a dozen that day. Although the meeting was going fine, there were several folks with and several without their video on. Some had called in, while others simply had it off. Well, on this occasion, one of the participants who was not on video made a rather harsh and pointed comment. The participant was well-thought-of, a leader of the group, and a step above most of the folks on the call as it pertains to hierarchy in the organization. I could see that the attendees with video on were visibly taken aback, some more than others. Many in the group began backpedaling on their ideas in response.*

Ultimately, we decided to move forward, but the participant who made the harshly pointed and challenging comment said very little as everyone worked to revise the plan and set appropriate objectives for the project. The meeting adjourned. About an hour later, I received an email from the critical participant who caused the stir on the call. It simply said, 'Did people not realize I was joking?'"

Observation #2: *"On another occasion, with a different team of folks, I was on a call. Same as before, some were on video, some on their phones, and some with the camera off. This was a larger group, and the software we were using showed people with video enabled on the first screen and those who did not have their video on populating subsequent pages or screens. As the meeting got underway, I, along with the other folks who could actually see each other on the screen, started tackling the agenda at hand. As we made decisions, discussed matters, and worked through the agenda, there was an audible* Hmph! *that seemed to come out of nowhere. It was only then that I realized that while the on-camera people were engaged, others were not, and we had essentially forgotten all about them."*

Perhaps you have had similar experiences, both as the attendees on camera or as one of the attendees off camera. When you are off camera, sarcasm, hand gestures, and other nonverbal cues are unavailable to the rest of the meeting participants. This can lead to confusion, misunderstanding, and even a loss of trust. Furthermore, the people on camera tend to get more attention, or even worse, they forget their fellow attendees off camera even exist. Out of sight, out of mind.

The purpose of this chapter is to emphasize something that we've been underscoring all along. One of the biggest opportunities of virtual meetings lies in simply embracing video – allowing it to be a window into the meeting and others' lives (or dining rooms). Let the richer communication medium allow for richer communication.

In this chapter, we will explore:

- The reasons for seriously turning on the video *every time*.
- Some of the nuances of media richness theory.
- The reality of Zoom fatigue.
- How to motivate others to turn on their video.

Differences in Meeting Satisfaction and Effectiveness by Modality

As we seek to make data-driven decisions related to *meeting effectiveness*, allow us to share some important findings culled from recent data Joe and colleagues collected showing substantial reasons for being on-camera in our virtual meetings.

The first table below compares *meeting satisfaction* in terms of format both before and after the pandemic. As a reminder, hybrid meetings are some combination of telephone, video, and face-to-face (e.g. two people in a room videoconferencing with two people in another room in another country). Before COVID-19, face-to-face meetings were the highest rated in terms of satisfaction, with video and hybrid formats coming in close behind. COVID-19 hit, and hybrid and video meeting satisfaction increased dramatically with teleconference and face-to-face lagging behind. Partly, these results are due to preferences pre-COVID-19, while part of it can be attributed to the necessity for adjustments during COVID-19. All of these results are on a five-point scale, with 1 being least satisfying and 5 being most satisfying.

Meeting Satisfaction

Format Style	October 2019	May 2020
Face-to-Face	3.38	3.23
Telephone	3.09	3.41
Video	3.34	3.52
Hybrid	3.21	3.67

What really was surprising is best displayed in the next table on meeting effectiveness before COVID-19 and in the midst of the pandemic. In terms of meeting effectiveness, before COVID-19, face-to-face and hybrid meetings were found to be most effective, with video and teleconference coming in behind. Then, with COVID-19 and the forced transition to virtual meetings, virtual and hybrid jumped ahead, followed by face-to-face and teleconference. As before, all these numbers are on a five-point scale and show that generally speaking, most people give their meetings a "meh" rating. They rate them all only slightly better than neutral, suggesting that, sadly, our meetings are on average, slightly better than neutral. It's as though we are all okay with simply receiving a participation prize, and somewhat less willing to engage in the effort to make meetings effective.

Meeting Effectiveness

Format Style	October 2019	May 2020
Face-to-Face	3.54	3.70
Telephone	3.14	3.67
Video	3.32	3.82
Hybrid	3.50	3.89

What's Wrong with Teleconferences?

One observation that you may have already noticed is the consistently low results for teleconferences. In fact, you may even wonder, "Why are teleconferences consistently less than others in terms of satisfaction and effectiveness?" It is because when you are on a teleconference, you are anonymous. Think of your last teleconference. How many times did someone say, "I didn't catch that. Can you repeat?" Sadly, we know the translation of that statement: "I wasn't paying attention to the meeting, and now I'm asking you to catch me up so I can sound intelligent in front of the boss."

The problem with the teleconference meeting is that the anonymity practically invites multitasking, which is really another word for inattention. The things that distract us during teleconference meetings (e.g. texting, emailing, posting on social media, looking at cat pictures, grocery shopping, etc.) are all available at our fingertips. We cannot help ourselves and may justify this as extra productivity that does not harm the meeting. However, most of the recent research on multitasking indicates that it cannot be done effectively. A *Harvard Business Review* article by Atchley (2010) perhaps stated it best in the title: "You can't multitask, so stop trying." Other, more recent studies showed that having a laptop in a lecture or meeting makes for more distraction and less retention of the content in general (Dynarski 2017). Thus, teleconferences DO NOT WORK.

Videoconferencing and hybrid meetings where video is on are less anonymous. It is harder to check-out in virtual meetings when your video is on because people can tell when you are distracted, not paying attention, or working on something else, and people call each other out. That keeps everyone on their game in a video conference meeting.

The numbers also show that video conference meetings are as good or better than face-to-face meetings, which were considered the gold standard pre–COVID-19. The reason they are so similar in

111

rating is that they are so similar in context. With face-to-face and video, you can see the person and read their nonverbal cues. That is, you can see them roll their eyes when they say something that is supposed to be dripping with sarcasm. Absent of those cues, you might end up in a meeting like Joe described at the beginning of this chapter, scrambling to respond to a "joke."

The Case for Making Every Virtual Meeting a *Video* Meeting

Based on the data presented earlier in this chapter, you might conclude that video is a good idea for most virtual meetings, but it's still okay to use the other formats when necessary. Although generally true, we make the case here that the choice of format must be dependent upon the nature of the message being sent and received. The more complex the message, the richer the format needs to be to allow for the transmission of that message.

We alluded to this in Chapter 2 when we mentioned media richness theory as it relates to the ability to make deeper connections with our conversation partners when using video versus audio alone (Daft and Lengel 1986). Media richness theory is a framework used to describe a medium's ability to reproduce the information sent over it. For example, this theory could be used to describe how effective the telephone is for transmitting general dialogue and conversation versus transmitting the details contained in a photograph or spreadsheet of data. Note, however, that the telephone we are describing here is equivalent to a landline. We are not referring to the computer in your hand (i.e. an iPhone does not equal a telephone).

Media richness theory essentially claims that richer personal communication media are generally more effective for communicating complex issues in comparison to leaner, less rich media (e.g. email, text, or phone). In other words, if you are planning a meeting that will require extensive discussion, debate, consideration of alternatives, problem-solving, and/or decision-making, lean media is *not* a good option.

When deciding what communication medium to use for a given message or meeting, the primary factor should be to reduce equivocality, in other words, the possibility of misinterpretations *or* multiple interpretations of a message. The more likely a message is to be challenging to decode and understand, the more cues and data will be needed to interpret it correctly. For example, scheduling a meeting is typically fairly straightforward and can be done via email, a lean form of media. But a detailed message about a person's work performance on a recent project probably needs a richer medium, such as a face-to-face meeting.

But wait, there's a pandemic. Or, hopefully, in the future, it's simply that the person is across town, across the state, across the country, or perhaps on another continent, and you still need to communicate a complex problem or detailed message. In that case, you could use the telephone, which has wonderful auditory cues. However, the better option would be the richer medium, or a virtual meeting using your preferred video conference platform.

We must admit that the face-to-face meeting is still a richer medium than the virtual meeting. In face-to-face meetings, you can manipulate objects together (e.g. engineering project), you can see all the nonverbal cues, and you can even engage in approach touch behaviors, such as handshakes to signify agreement to a deal. Although the COVID-19 world makes us think twice about coming within six feet of anyone, there will likely come a time when face-to-face meetings will resume in earnest and this richest of meeting medium will be available once more.

Until that time, video allows for more "best practices" in interpersonal communication than teleconferencing can ever allow. Thus, we strongly encourage everyone to *turn on the camera now!*

Caveats to *Every* Virtual Meeting as a Video Meeting

Now, even though we agree and are strong in our push to encourage everyone to turn on their camera in their virtual meetings, that recommendation does not come without a major caveat that must be attended to and discussed here. First, "Zoom fatigue" is real. As early as April, articles from trusted news and research-oriented sources started exclaiming all the virtual meetings were sapping all of our energy and drive for work in general (Fosslien and Duffy 2020). Liz Fosslien and Mollie West Duffy described the issue of Zoom fatigue and several ways to combat the exhaustion, including avoiding multitasking (sound familiar?), taking breaks, and so on. By May 2020, it was no longer "What is this thing?" and had transitioned to articles titled "Zoom fatigue is real – here's why video calls are so draining" (Sander and Bauman 2020). Libby Sander and Oliver Bauman identified five reasons why they are so draining, as follows:

1. We miss out on a lot of nonverbal communication. During videoconferencing, you have to pay a lot more attention to catch the nonverbal communication that you naturally can attend to in face-to-face meetings with your peripheral vision and auditory signals.

2. What if the kids run in? We feel anxious about our home, our space, our cat, or our kids being a distraction. All of that makes us on edge during the meetings.

3. No water-cooler catchups. We don't get to catch up, talk shop, or even small-talk between or around the meetings. It's all work and all on, all the time.

4. Looking at our own face is stressful. As pleasant as our faces might be, looking at oneself and being one's own worst critic

angry customer when we'd just like to tell them how we really feel. Or showing enthusiasm for an idea the boss just proposed that you know is probably not going to work and you'll be blamed. Nod and smile, nod and smile.

Pre–COVID-19, we all engaged in relatively minimal emotional labor and surface acting in our meetings. Studies showed that those behaviors would spike during meetings with the boss or the boss's boss (Shumski Thomas et al. 2018). But, generally speaking, when asked whether we would "fake an appropriate expression" during a meeting, we usually said we would not. Fast forward a few months, though, and suddenly, across *all* meeting formats, we see about a standard deviation increase in the frequency of surface acting in meetings. Instead of generally not doing much surface acting, we, on average, began doing it substantially more in all our meetings.

SURFACE ACTING

Format Style	October 2019	May 2020
Face-to-Face	2.36	3.14
Telephone	2.09	2.57
Video	2.18	2.79
Hybrid	2.12	2.29

What does that mean? Well, of all the types of emotional labor, surface acting is the most harmful. It is connected with both psychological and physical harm. People who do a lot of surface acting experience more burnout on average compared to those who do not. Burnout is a major predictor of quitting one's job, as well as depression, anxiety, and even suicidal ideation. So, in addition to a pandemic and all the wonderful things that come with it, let's add burnout induced by trying to hide our worries by engaging in surface acting.

This is why we strongly recommend engaging in *all* the best practices we previously discussed to reduce the overall meeting load, by making every meeting count. Even though it is true that we do more emotional labor now than we did before the pandemic, this is true across all meeting formats.

This is not a justification for keeping video off. Quite the contrary, choosing to *not* turn on the video does not actually make it much better. In fact, it makes it more likely you'll have a bad meeting, and as we've said before, all the evidence suggests that bad meetings beget more meetings, usually to fix the problems *caused* by the bad meeting. So, even as we caution about emotional labor, we strongly encourage video, because it will ensure a better meeting is possible.

Motivating Others to Turn on the Video

Hopefully by now you have been convinced to turn on your own video. Perhaps your team doesn't have a problem with video, and everyone turns on their camera. However, we know there are some holdouts. Perhaps you have one on your team or know of one on another team. Or perhaps you've noticed the trend that as the meeting gets larger, the number of people turning off their video grows. This may be due to a number of reasons like blaming tech failings, video cutting out, or bandwidth issues. It's a ready-made excuse to say, "Oh, I'm helping everyone by keeping my video off." However, if you are the one speaking, wouldn't you rather be able to get a sense of how your message is resonating by reading the nonverbals of your audience? One of the best ways you can "help" is to be an attentive attendee who can offer a nod of encouragement when listening to another person speak.

Here are a few ways to make the business case for video on and perhaps motivate those holding out:

1. First, the risks associated with technology failing are worth the potential reward. Video is anywhere from 5 to 25% better in terms of effectiveness than teleconference based on the data we've shared. Just making our meetings 5% better might actually mean one less meeting because of efficiency gains. It's simply worth the benefits, even if it means learning where the newfangled button is to turn on the built-in camera.

2. Second, as mentioned before, normalize the new view. If everyone is in the same boat while on video, turning on the camera is not so embarrassing. Allow the video to be a window into the lives of our colleagues. We might learn we have something in common, or perhaps just develop some empathy for the struggling working moms and dads with little ones learning at home during a pandemic.

3. Third, use positive peer pressure on the holdouts. If everyone else has their camera on and it's working, but one holdout remains, allow the positive peer pressure to occur and inspire a change in behavior. If that one camera stays in the off position, then have a dialogue with the holdout on a separate call, and discuss with them the reasons for not turning on video and ask why they are hesitant. More than likely they are concerned about the window into their messy or less-than-posh home. Or perhaps it's just camera fear. There are plenty of resources to tap into for helping people gain better confidence and competence on camera. In fact, this book provides a perfect starting point. See Chapter 6 for best practices for on-camera communication.

You may be thinking, "If I know the person really well, I don't need video. I can see their face in my mind's eye, which is as good as any camera, or better." Okay, sure, for quick, noncomplex conversations with people you know very well, yes, choose the less rich medium and do a voice call. But, if there is anyone on the call who does not know everyone else, the face-to-face or video meeting is always going to be better, for all the reasons we've discussed. Again, allow the purpose of the meeting to drive the choice of medium.

One way to determine whether it should be a video meeting, a phone call, or even just an email is to ask yourself this question: "Would the meeting in question likely have been a face-to-face meeting but can't be due to the pandemic or other reasons?" If the answer is yes, then opt for a video conference and make sure the webcam is on during that virtual meeting. If the meeting would have been simply a phone call, like a quick check-in with a colleague, then a phone call will suffice even in a post–COVID-19 world.

Case Study: Video Meeting Converts at the Executive Level

Summit Leadership Partners is a leadership and organizational performance consultancy based in Charlotte, North Carolina. Summit partners with investors, boards, CEOs, and management teams to accelerate organization performance in companies all over the globe. Much of their work during 2020 focused on helping leaders adapt to the remote world, and one of the very immediate needs was a revamp of meeting protocols.

According to Dan Hawkins, Summit's founder and CEO, "At the beginning, most of our executives were doing teleconferences and no video, and now almost all of them are making it a requirement that their management meetings are all video."

Why the move to a mandate for webcam on? Hawkins pointed to the fact that many meetings without video were unproductive or, worse yet, resulted in leaders missing some important clues. "I've seen some meetings go bad where nothing is resolved, and they realize they have to be more attentive to this. I think bad sessions gone wrong have stretched new muscles."

Those new muscles mean being more attentive to meeting dynamics than ever before. If someone has not spoken up much during a meeting, leaders are more apt to draw them out and ask them to weigh in to ensure there is true alignment and support. In an in-person meeting, it is easier to read the room and get a sense of who is on board and who is not. In a virtual setting, leaders recognize the need to take full inventory during the meeting itself because there's less opportunity to pop into someone's office down the hall to check in afterward.

Dan has also seen a change in the structure of meetings as well. Rather than a four-hour staff meeting or a two-hour town hall, leaders will have more shorter, in-the-moment meetings that focus on one topic. The purpose of the meeting is stated upfront. Is this meeting to inform, debate, or decide? It allows all to know what is expected during the session and helps the leader to track the meeting to a specific outcome. Before wrapping up, leaders are being even more intentional about another communication best practice – publishing action items, owners, and next steps. One positive outcome of the pandemic, according to Hawkins, is that "it's definitely raising the bar on meeting discipline."

The more frequent but shorter meetings may also be indicative of another consequence of working remote. Hawkins says, "I think people are lonely working out of their homes all day." Those video meetings allow for some human connection that is harder to come by during a pandemic.

Conclusion

At this point, we hope we have sufficiently built a business case for making (almost) every virtual meeting a video meeting. Although we gladly acknowledge times when video may not be possible (e.g. internet bandwidth issues), the benefits greatly outstrip the drawbacks of using the video tool. And those benefits go well beyond the improvements in meeting satisfaction and effectiveness. It humanizes our colleagues in ways that further augment cohesion and collaboration and perhaps most importantly, drive engagement. That's the topic of our next chapter, but before we leave this topic, one more pep talk. Video is your friend! Use it!

Chapter Takeaways

- We all have experiences where things get "lost in translation" during a meeting where nonverbal cues or verbal cues are misread.
- Face-to-face meetings and virtual meetings are essentially equal in terms of overall meeting satisfaction and effectiveness, and telephone/teleconference meetings are the worst.
- The medium we choose constrains the complexity with which we can communicate, so in general, choose a meeting format with a rich medium (i.e. virtual meetings are a go!).
- Zoom fatigue is real. It's caused by the emotional labor we do naturally when working with other people, but good meetings can reduce the burden.
- There are meaningful ways to motivate others to make *every* meeting a *video* meeting.

References

Atchley, Paul. 2010. "You can't multitask, so stop trying." *Harvard Business Review*. https://hbr.org/2010/12/you-cant-multi-task-so-stop-tr

Daft, Richard L., and Robert H Lengel. 1986. "Organizational information requirements, media richness and structural design." *Management Science* 32 (5): 554–571.

Dynarski, Susan. 2017. "Laptops are great. But not during a lecture or a meeting." *The New York Times* November 22, 2017.

Fosslien, Liz, and Mollie West Duffy. 2020. "How to combat zoom fatigue." *Harvard Business Review*. https://hbr.org/2020/04/how-to-combat-zoom-fatigue.

Sander, Libby, and Oliver Bauman. 2020. "Zoom fatigue is real — here's why video calls are so draining." *Ideas.Ted.Com*. https://ideas.ted.com/zoom-fatigue-is-real-heres-why-video-calls-are-so-draining/.

Shumski Thomas, Jane, Jessie L Olien, Joseph A Allen, Steven G Rogelberg, and John E Kello. 2018. "Faking it for the higher-ups: Status and surface acting in workplace meetings." *Group & Organization Management* 43 (1): 72–100.

Chapter 8

Driving Engagement in a Virtual Meeting

The Converged Perspective

F or the vast majority of industries, the sudden shift to remote work was incredibly challenging, but perhaps even more so for those businesses that were gearing up for a product launch. Such was the challenge for one of Karin's clients that found itself in an unusual position.

A Story from Karin's Perspective

It was years in the making. Meticulous research, testing, and vetting had led to a product that was finally ready to be brought to market. The team brought in to lead the launch was a seasoned one with decades of experience in the industry, but the final planning stages of the go-to-market strategy were taking place at a time like no other. It was mid-2020, and the playbook for what was expected to be largely a virtual launch had yet to be written.

Even the hiring process for the sales force was markedly different, with virtual video meetings replacing the "let me walk you through my résumé" discussion typically had in person. However, scaling up might have been the easy part. The real challenge? Training hundreds of people on everything they needed to know without the benefit of in-person sessions in a highly regulated industry. The stakes were indeed high.

Any training professional faced a similar challenge with a complete conversion to virtual delivery – for Karin's client, how do you keep hundreds of new salespeople engaged so that they actually learn what they need to learn?

But this challenge goes far beyond the training use case mentioned here. The hallmark of a productive virtual meeting is *engagement*, which is shorthand for a back-and-forth sharing of ideas or troubleshooting of problems that moves the needle.

Driving engagement in remote meetings requires a change in tactics, a strategic approach, and more effort on the part of the facilitator to drive results. In the following pages, we will look at some best practices based in science as well as real-world success stories that you can use as a blueprint to make your own virtual meetings a dialogue rather than a monologue.

In this chapter, we will explore:

- Why getting people to engage is so hard.
- The science behind engaging employees during meetings.
- Strategies to employ before the meeting even begins.
- How to encourage webcam use by others.
- Why a linear approach to a meeting won't work.
- Why strong facilitation skills are critical for success.
- How to leverage engagement tools on the platform.

Fighting the Default Position

Think about how you typically interact with a screen. You watch TV. You take in a movie while sitting quietly in a theater. You read the latest news on your smartphone. We have been conditioned to be observers and largely passive observers at that. This is the default position that we all typically assume when we are interacting (or rather not interacting) with screens. So, it should come as no surprise that when we want people to be engaged in a virtual meeting, it feels like we are pulling teeth. Our minds want to stay fixed in that observer mode, but for a virtual meeting to be productive, all attendees need to move into active participant mode.

We have to learn how to "flip the script" quite literally. According to psychological and communication science, people develop schemas and scripts for how interactions and activities progress (Singer and Salovey 1991). For example, when you walk in the door to a home and see balloons, streamers, and confetti all over the entryway, you might immediately think, "Someone's having a party." Then, you notice the pile of presents on a table, a banner that says "Happy 39th, um, You Know, Again." And then you know this is a birthday party for someone who is "39" again. This is a schema for a typical birthday, and so it would not surprise you if singing broke out, along with plates of cake and ice cream being passed around.

Well, just as we have a script or schema around what is expected with birthday parties, we have the same thing with movie theaters, church services, gas stations, and even what happens when we turn on our computer, tablet, laptop, or other device. The schema pre–COVID-19 for many folks was consumer of information, observer, and perhaps keyboard pounder. Because we are used to that script, interacting with a little box sitting on top of your screen or laptop as though it's a person is, well, kind of weird. Or at least it was.

Therefore, the way most people approach a virtual meeting doesn't help. They often focus on their own agendas and sharing the information they want to share without considering if their content is actually sticking. They let their audiences off the "attention hook" by not even attempting to get them engaged and allowing them to simply be observers without any expectation that they have to do anything but be present and accounted for. However, if what is being communicated on the screen isn't captivating – or even more interesting than what is going on outside their home office windows – minds will wander, the message will be lost, and communication is brought to a screeching halt.

Making virtual meetings engaging requires a different approach and breaking out of the script, but the approach is steeped in best practices in meeting science.

Meetings and Engagement: Joe's Origin Story

Some years ago, Joe completed his dissertation work related to meeting science. Specifically, he sought to understand what a manager could do not only to make their meetings better but to have people engage, both in the meeting *and* outside of the meeting in their everyday work.

But what do we mean by employee engagement? From a meeting scientist's perspective, it's the degree to which workers pour their whole selves into the work, allowing for greater effort, dedication, and even the end state of becoming fully absorbed in the work (Kahn 1990). We also know that an engaged workforce is a high-performing workforce (Allen and Rogelberg 2013). In fact, evidence suggests that an engaged workforce may actually work 25% harder than a nonengaged or disengaged workforce (Mackay, Allen, and Landis 2017). This is to say, that if meetings could be leveraged to create an engaged workforce during and after meetings, it was worth exploring.

Through Joe's research, he discovered three key things a manager can do to enable the psychological conditions for employee engagement, thereby engaging employees in the meeting *and* in their work.

Using a time-ordered survey design (e.g. take one survey and then another a few weeks later), his model proved to be a wonderful starting point for what's proven to be a fruitful area of meeting science. With a few more details than was shared in Chapter 3, here are the three key things a manager can do to promote engagement during and after meetings:

1. **Make the meetings relevant.** Meeting relevance refers to the degree to which the purpose and aims of the meeting matter to those in the meeting. When they do, people participate in the meeting, they engage in the meeting, and the results of the meeting often further engage them afterward. Have you ever sat in a meeting and thought, "Why am I here?" Unless you were having an existential crisis, more than likely the issue was that the meeting was irrelevant to your current situation, needs, and set of tasks. Thus, it was distracting you from your work rather than enabling or engaging you.

2. **Provide voice opportunities in meetings.** Voice in meetings refers to the feeling that one can speak up in the meeting, be heard, and have his/her opinions acknowledged, and in some cases, accepted, validated, and used in the decision-making process. This is a manifestation of meetings that are truly psychologically safe. People feel that they can share their thoughts, feelings, and ideas, without retaliation from either the meeting leader or their fellow attendees.

3. **Manage the meeting effectively from a time perspective.** Meeting time courtesy refers to the degree to which the meeting starts and ends on time, and the meeting process is managed effectively so as to optimize the time to accomplish the goals, aims, and agenda of the meeting. Surprisingly, this was by far the most predictive manager behavior of *all* the

127

conditions of engagement and overall employee engagement. People like knowing that their time is managed carefully, and thus some meeting scientists refer to this set of behaviors as an effective "steward" of other people's time.

Taken together, these three behaviors, which are primarily encouraged by the meeting leader and partially required by the meeting attendee, have the potential to engage folks in the meeting and afterwards. And although this was one of Joe's earliest works in meeting science, it remains one of the more influential over time. Why? Because it verifies that the science *can* and *should* impact the overall performance of employees and their organizations.

Engaging Meetings in the Virtual World

As you might suspect, all of the elements of engagement are appropriate for the virtual environment and none of them are exclusive to only face-to-face settings. In other words, once again, old meeting science is relevant to the new virtual meeting world. However, how you bake them into your virtual meeting best practices can be tricky if you do not make the effort to adjust your approach before, during, and after the meeting. Let's translate the three key ingredients of any meeting into the recipe for an engaging virtual version.

Make the Meeting Relevant: Fighting the "Less Than" Mentality

One of the benefits of scheduling meetings in an all-remote world is the logistical ease of doing so. Setting up a meeting can take no more than creating a calendar invite with the link to the platform and sending it off to potential attendees. Contrast this with an in-person meeting, which often requires negotiating with busy schedules to block off enough time to bring everyone together, finding and reserving a space, and arranging travel to and from if necessary.

The relatively minimal effort it takes to set up a virtual meeting, however, can have an impact on how the meeting is viewed and sometimes whether it even happens at all. Canceling plans to fly somewhere is a much more consequential task than simply changing your attendance response on the event from "yes" to "no." Getting people to commit to showing up for the virtual meeting is critical and goes back to Joe's first key finding. If you don't make the meeting relevant, you run the risk of not having the meeting at all.

What can you do to combat this potential lack of follow-through? Go beyond just the automated calendar invite.

Prior to the meeting, provide a framework for what will be discussed, get attendees invested in the content that will be covered, and provide a compelling objective for why they want to take the time to meet. Sure, if you are the boss, perhaps you can demand attendance, but that does not guarantee that your team is mentally engaged even if they show up on the screen. An agenda with enough specificity can spark interest, inspire attendees to adequately prepare, and raise the priority level of the meeting itself on busy calendars (Cohen et al. 2011). If you are in a position to do so, consider assigning agenda items to individuals on your team, which will help them become even more invested in attending because they have a job to do (Mroz et al. 2018).

Break Down Tech Barriers

With the multitude of virtual meeting platforms, there may be additional barriers to engagement that you can easily address ahead of time as well, such as a lack of familiarity with the particular videoconferencing tool being used. You may be very comfortable using Microsoft Teams but when you send that invitation to an external stakeholder who prefers GoToMeeting, you may run into problems.

Consider adding this best practice to your virtual meeting routine when sending an invitation to someone outside of your organization. In the invitation, include a link to either a video tutorial or a text article that discusses "How to Get Started" on the platform you plan to use. It may not relieve all of their concerns over using a new tool, but it at least gives them quick access to information that can help them navigate it better from the get-go.

Another best practice is to always have a backup plan for a technology snafu. Don't just give them one way to connect. Make sure you give them dial-in numbers so there are multiple ways to let the show go on . . . even if it's just an audio-only version. After all, what can go wrong, will go wrong, so being prepared for tech challenges is just good business practice.

A surefire way to suffer massive losses of engagement is to spend too much time troubleshooting the tech once the meeting is underway. Let's say your conversation partner's internet connection starts to flag. The situation may be temporary, so it may be worth pausing for a moment or two to see if stability returns. However, anything longer than a minute or so starts to sap all of the energy from the meeting. The first line of defense is to suggest the person with the wavering signal log out and then log back in. However, if the connection trouble doesn't go away even with the second log-in, cut your losses. Suggest that person dial in or, if it's a one-on-one meeting, determine if you want to reschedule or move the meeting to a phone call.

Setting the Engagement Stage

As we have been underscoring throughout the book, one of the critical determinants of virtual meeting success is whether video is being used by participants. As a leader of a team, you may be able to mandate the camera be on, but it's nearly impossible to force someone's hand outside of your organization. But that doesn't mean you are powerless to affect their behavior on that front.

TRY THIS: For Your Next Meeting

In our experiences, these two techniques have found a high level of success in actually prompting people to turn their cameras on:

1. In the email or calendar invite you send prior to the meeting, let your attendees know you are planning to turn your video on and give them the reasons why. A few options:

    a. I like to put a name with a face.

    b. I find that my video meetings are more productive than those when I don't turn my video on.

    c. I find that video helps me to pay better attention.

    If you make the case for why video is important to you, it may encourage them to consider why it might be beneficial for them, too. At a minimum, it puts them on notice that you will be showing up with the webcam on. Hopefully, they'll return the favor.

2. Once you are in a meeting, make a small ask. Explain to your attendees that one of the things you have really missed with the shift to mostly (if not all) remote is the ability to see people. You can ask them if they'd be okay turning on their webcam briefly, so you can at least see their faces, then let them know it's perfectly fine for them to turn it off if they do not feel comfortable. Sometimes making the request a small one will prompt them to turn the camera on. In essence, though, it rips off the Band-aid, and people are likely to keep the camera on from that point on.

Think Dynamic, Not Linear

As you learned during our chapter on meeting best practices, constructing and distributing an agenda is an essential step. Perhaps each agenda item is assigned to a different member of the team who prepares a presentation on that topic. However, in a virtual meeting, those presentations can lead to pitfalls in meeting effectiveness.

Typically, presenters in a remote meeting think in very linear terms. They start with an introduction of their assigned topic, move into screen share mode, methodically walk through their slides, and eventually end the formal presentation segment by asking, "Are there any questions?" Maybe someone might have had a question about something from the second slide, but by the time the speaker wrapped up the thirtieth slide, that question had probably evaporated into the air that had grown increasingly more stale as the presentation wore on.

Joe's research has revealed that voice opportunities, or the chance for participants to provide input, ask questions, and make comments, are a key component of any meeting but are especially valuable in a virtual setting. With that in mind, consider this: rather than simply presenting in a long stream of slides, break things up to avoid disengagement. Take this tip from Joe's classroom. He breaks up his lectures into "lecturettes" of no longer than seven minutes so that questions can be answered, activities engaged in, and so forth.

Distraction Danger in Screen Share

When we appear in the *Brady Bunch* boxes or gallery view during a virtual meeting, the lens does hold us accountable for our behavior. Provided that the meeting is small enough, we can quickly identify who's paying attention. However, when anyone shares his or her screen and displays slides, a demo, or a document, the content usually takes over the majority of the on-screen real estate. The people boxes may still be visible, but they've been diminished.

This format presents a challenge from an engagement perspective. Online presenters tend to become a runaway train, plowing through their content in order to get from point A to point B without considering who is along for the ride. But without regular check-ins along the way, a presenter may find all passengers have lost interest by the time they get to the final destination.

Without the camera forcing people to at least appear attentive, it is very easy for attendees to tune out. The longer a presenter spends in screen share, the more at risk she/he is of losing the audience's attention. However, there is a simple technique that can help prevent it: move in and out of screen share.

Rather than structuring your presentation to be a quick introduction, a walk through the slides, and Q&A at the end, chunk your content into digestible segments and stop after each segment to ask for input or take questions. For example, if you have thirty minutes of content to present, break the presentation up into three segments (e.g. 10 minutes each) and pause after each segment for Q&A. However, just stopping to ask for questions will likely not elicit the engagement you are hoping for.

At each pause point, stop sharing your screen and allow the switch to full gallery view. When participants see themselves and/or fellow meeting attendees take over the majority of the screen once again, it immediately reengages them. You've changed their on-screen environment and that change pulls them back to attention. By taking away the slides or other content that you may have been sharing off their screens, you force them to focus on what is being said and remove the "resting place" of the slide which they may have been staring at but not necessarily digesting.

This jumping out of screen share primes them for participation and gives you a much better chance of getting them to share their own thoughts and opinions.

Strong Facilitation Is a Must

Conversations in a virtual world can be clunky. Without the benefit of reading body language in a robust way or hearing the intake of air of someone beside you who is about to speak, it can be difficult to know who wants to speak when. So, if you try to hold a free-flowing dialogue in a virtual meeting without strong moderation, you likely end up with a mess. People talk over each other with only segments of sentences making it through. Two people speak at once and then realizing the faux pas, they both stop talking and wait . . . until they both attempt to speak again at the same time. The disjointed dialogue leads to frustration and poor outcomes for all. Given these limitations, the role of the facilitator becomes even more important in a virtual meeting, and can make or break the meeting's success.

Provide Ground Rules

Meeting science supports the use of ground rules in *all* meeting situations, and virtual meetings are not an exception (Allen, Rogelberg, and Scott 2008). At the outset of the meeting, the facilitator should let attendees know their input is not only appreciated but expected. However, in a virtual meeting, it is the job of the moderator to let attendees know how to present their thoughts. If the platform you are using includes a chat function, let them know this can serve as a parking lot for their questions, comments, and ideas. Some people will feel more comfortable providing input in this manner rather than verbalizing it. Don't just let the chat thread go unattended. If the expectation was set that chat is part of the conversation, make sure it is visited on a regular basis and any comments be addressed and worked into the discussion.

If there are more than a few people on a call, ask participants to somehow identify themselves as they speak. This can be as simple as stating their names ("This is Sarah . . ."). This allows others on the call to immediately connect the comment with the person speaking and perhaps even more easily find their video box on the screen.

In person, someone can easily ask for permission to speak by raising his hand. This can be done virtually as well. Some platforms allow for participants to click a hand-raising icon, which will appear on the screen as a signal to the moderator that they would like to talk. If the meeting is small enough, the facilitator can go old school and ask people to physically raise their hands if their video is on. That movement within the frame is easily detectable.

Read the Virtual Room

While video does provide at least some visual feedback, it is still more difficult to read the room in a virtual meeting. That task becomes even more arduous when the boxes are minimized in screen share mode. That's why it is critical for facilitators to use the gallery view to maximize the size of those participant boxes. The bigger the box, the easier it'll be to read body language and pick up on visual cues to indicate someone has something to say.

As a moderator, it's your job to direct the flow of conversation in a way that makes it as fluid as possible, and one way to better ensure that is to ask for input by name. One of the reasons why online discussions are choppy is the fact that individuals don't know when they truly have the floor. The meeting leader can eliminate the uncertainty by verbalizing who has the voice opportunity in the moment.

For example, let's say two people speak at the same time but both sheepishly pause when they realize they are stepping on each other's toes. The moderator could let them do the awkward "You go first . . . no, *you* go first" routine *or* just make the decision and say, "Bob, why don't you speak and then Candace, you can follow." It's not a matter of playing favorites. Bob's input isn't any more valuable than Candace's, but this phrase lets each person know when it is their turn to talk.

Another way to guide the conversation is to look for visual cues that indicate someone has something to say. A dead giveaway is if someone unmutes herself. At that point, you can be fairly confident that a person has something to add, but she may still be unsure when to chime in. A strong facilitator will step in as soon as the unmuting occurs and make a formal invitation for that person to speak up. "Brenda, did you have something you wanted to say?"

One more visual cue to scan for is if someone leans toward the camera. That physical act of moving forward typically is a precursor of engagement. If you see someone leaning in, feel free to invite that person to take the floor. Now, this is not foolproof. That person may have just needed to adjust his position for the sake of comfort. However, the benefits of being proactive outweigh any fleeting discomfort the participant may feel being singled out.

Make sure you allot enough time to read the room as well. As we discussed in Chapter 6, a pause in virtual meetings can feel very pronounced, but scanning the screen and looking for nonverbal nuances takes time if done with intentionality. Plus, if you are working with a global team or customers, those pauses become even more important. According to Erin Meyer, author of *The Culture Map*, if participants are from a "high comfort with silence" culture (e.g. Japan, Indonesia, or China), they may have not only a tolerance for silence but also an expectation of a longer pause (up to eight seconds in China) before they speak (Meyer 2019). If you don't pause long enough, you may not provide enough space for people from "high comfort with silence" cultures to speak up.

Ideally, as a moderator, you will seek to pull out even participation from all, whether it be through giving people the floor when you spot verbal cues or inviting people to weigh in if you've noticed someone's voice has not been heard. The meeting experience will be richer for all and the outcome will be improved thanks to a deliberate effort to keep all engaged and allow everyone to have a voice.

Watch the Clock

No one will be upset if your meeting goes short. Everyone will be upset if it goes long (van Eerde and Azar 2020). That's why a strong facilitator must mind the agenda and move things along accordingly. As Joe's seminal research discovered, effective time management is a key indicator for meeting success. However, in an all-remote world, it takes on even more significance.

Many people are juggling unexpected childcare, homeschooling, or caregiving with their work priorities. Being respectful of their at-home demands means keeping the meeting to the time allocated. That funny cat video can be shared at another time – that is, unless the agenda contained a line item for "funny cat videos."

In fact, new research tells us that being good stewards of others' time in meetings includes *both* the front and back end of the meeting. Meetings need to start on time because late meetings are much worse than on-time meetings (Allen, Lehmann-Willenbrock, and Rogelberg 2018) *and* people need at least five minutes to recover and cognitively transition after a good meeting (Knowles and Allen 2020). The best meeting leaders and attendees ensure that awareness of the clock translates into starting and ending on time.

Leverage Engagement Tools on the Platform

One of the best techniques to keep people engaged is to make attendees *do* something. It forces them from that passive role to an active one that drives better meeting outcomes. Thankfully, many virtual meeting platforms have tools you can use to do just that.

Polling

For meetings larger than a handful of people, polling participants can be an effective device. Not only can you get a quick snapshot of information, but you also move people to take part in the meeting itself. Most platforms allow you to load the questions when you set up the meeting itself, but some will also allow you to create them on the fly. Typically, only the host can see the answers arrive in real-time, but settings can be adjusted to allow for all to see answers tally up in the moment. If you are controlling the poll, make sure you give attendees enough time to register their responses. Once all have weighed in, you can share the results and use them as a launching point for further discussion.

Breakout Rooms

When the world was more of a colocated one, huddle rooms – i.e. small group conference rooms – were a common sight in offices. Many videoconferencing platforms have created the virtual version of those huddle rooms through breakout rooms.

Breakout rooms allow the leader to take a large meeting and divide it into smaller ones by assigning participants to different virtual spaces. Breakout room participants can be assigned to a particular one in advance (by project team, for example) or placed randomly during the actual meeting when the host creates a certain number of breakout rooms with an equal number of people. The platform determines who goes where.

Consistent with meeting and group science, these breakout rooms allow for the optimum meeting size to be achieved (Landowski et al. 2019). Most research indicates that for meetings where collaborative decision-making is to occur, the optimal meeting size is around five to seven individuals. For most problems, that number allows for adequate diversity in terms of expertise while keeping the group small enough to allow everyone to join in the conversation.

Therefore, these virtual huddle rooms provide dynamism to the meeting by changing things up for participants. It allows for easier conversation and participation due to the smaller size of the meeting itself and transitions what may have been a more formal meeting into a more informal opportunity to engage. The host of the meeting has the ability to broadcast messages to everyone through chat, which can include guidance for the small-group work or notifications on how much time is left.

A common use case for breakout rooms is for brainstorming. Each group is asked to come up with ideas for a particular initiative, usually for a limited period of time. Once that time is up, the host can close the breakout rooms and bring everyone back to the main meeting. At that point, the host can ask a representative of each group to present their ideas verbally or to write them in the chat as the basis for further discussion.

Case Study: Staying Engaged – A Participant Perspective

You may have heard of "The COVID 19." No, not the virus, but rather the weight gain many of us have experienced as a result of the pandemic.

But have you heard of "COVID Collarbone"?

That phrase was coined by Shannon Heath, a corporate and executive communications veteran at SAS Institute, the world's leading AI and advanced analytics software platform. In her role, Shannon is used to spinning many plates while juggling metaphorical tiki torches – without allowing one plate or tiki torch to fall to the ground. But the move to remote work rocked her world – initially leading her to feel isolated and anxious without that near-daily in-person interaction.

Like many knowledge workers, virtual meetings started dominating her day, at first without video but soon with the webcam on. However, the notifications that kept popping up on her phone and multiple monitors (not to mention the challenge of online schooling for her little ones) were constant distractions.

To combat the stress, Shannon started taking short strolls to get some fresh air and simply escape the confines of her home office (a repurposed spare bedroom). Those strolls became longer walks, then jogs, and then multiple-mile runs. Strapping on her running shoes and heading outside became a part of her daily routine, which she then incorporated into her work meeting protocol. If it was a call before 10 a.m., her team knew she was likely to be taking it from the park as long as she didn't need to take notes or be on camera.

In the virtual video world, we have all become talking heads of a sort. Our coworkers see us typically from maybe mid-chest up. Such was the case for Shannon when one of her colleagues asked her on a more casual call, "Have you lost weight?" Shannon was delighted that someone noticed and answered in the affirmative, but wondered how her friend detected the change. Her response? "In our team call the other day, I noticed that your collarbone looks thinner."

Shannon laughs about what she calls "COVID Collarbone," but that wasn't the only change that Shannon noticed. When she took her meetings while on the move, Shannon found she was more present, recalling, "I started realizing I was hearing more and I was responding more." Moreover, when she finished the call, she could ponder what was discussed and let her creativity flow freely.

The focus Shannon found also reshaped how she engaged during her virtual video meetings as well. Instead of allowing the pings on her phone or the pop-ups on her multiple monitors to distract her from the meeting at hand, she now shuts down her extra monitor and throws her phone on the bed, out of reach and out of mind.

But will these practices last once a return to campus is possible? Shannon believes her approach will follow her. "I'm going to take this with me when we actually go back to the office because I'm going to allow myself to unchain from the desk. It's so easy to only half-listen, especially if we have two or three monitors in front of us. We have instant messages popping up and you feel like everything is immediate. Most things do not require immediate attention and just serve to distract us from really being present in a meeting."

COVID Collarbone may be just the physical manifestation of a post-pandemic gift.

TRY THIS

As a meeting leader, you have many ways to drive engagement of attendees. Before your next meeting, take a look at this checklist as a reminder of the tools you have at your disposal.

MEETING ENGAGEMENT CHECKLIST

Competency	Engagement Criteria	Yes or No
Creating Commitment	Info is sent before the meeting to get attendees invested in the content	[ ] Yes [ ] No
Webcam Use	Set the engagement stage by encouraging video on	[ ] Yes [ ] No
Timing	Content is divided into "bite-sized" chunks with adequate breaks	[ ] Yes [ ] No

Engagement		
Competency	**Criteria**	**Yes or No**
Facilitation	Direction and facilitation are used to guide the conversation	[ ] Yes [ ] No
Engagement	Opportunities for dialogue and Q&A are provided and encouraged throughout	[ ] Yes [ ] No
Tools	Leverage platform tools to add dynamism to the meeting	[ ] Yes [ ] No
	TOTAL YES	[ ]

Conclusion

It is possible to move people from the role of observer to active participant, but it won't happen without real effort on the part of both the meeting leader as well as the attendees. However, setting expectations for participation, thoughtfully planning out engagement opportunities, and strong facilitation throughout can pay dividends in moving business forward and making the most of virtual meetings. Still, best intentions can be derailed by a lack of professional etiquette in a virtual meeting. That's what we will cover in Chapter 9.

Chapter Takeaways

- Meeting engagement requires people to move from the default position of passive observer to active participant.
- Make the meeting matter to participants. Get them invested in what will be discussed before the meeting takes place.
- Break down technology barriers by giving them simple instructions on how to use the platform.

- Encourage webcam use by letting them know in advance you plan to have yours on and offer the reasons why you consider it valuable.

- Create opportunities for engagement by frequently stopping for Q&A, addressing comments in chat, or soliciting input by name.

- Be a proactive facilitator by reading visual cues and inviting people to contribute when recognized.

- Leverage tools of engagement on the platform like polling and breakout rooms to add dynamism to the meeting.

References

Allen, Joseph A., Nale Lehmann-Willenbrock, and Steven G. Rogelberg. 2018. "Let's get this meeting started: Meeting lateness and actual meeting outcomes." *Journal of Organizational Behavior* 39 (8): 1008–1021.

Allen, Joseph A., and Steven G. Rogelberg. 2013. "Manager-led group meetings: A context for promoting employee engagement." *Group & Organization Management* 38 (5): 543–569.

Allen, Joseph A., Steven G. Rogelberg, and John C. Scott. 2008. *Mind Your Meetings: Improve Your Organization's Effectiveness One Meeting at a Time.* Psychology Faculty Publications. *University of Nebraska at Omaha.*

Cohen, Melissa A., Steven G. Rogelberg, Joseph A. Allen, and Alexandra Luong. 2011. "Meeting design characteristics and attendee perceptions of staff/team meeting quality." *Group Dynamics: Theory, Research, and Practice* 15 (1): 90.

Kahn, William A. 1990. "Psychological conditions of personal engagement and disengagement at work." *Academy of Management Journal* 33 (4): 692–724.

Knowles, S., and Joseph A. Allen. 2020. "Why am I so exhausted?: Exploring the meeting recovery syndrome." Interdisciplinary Network for Group Research's (INGRoup) 15th Annual Conference, Seattle, Washington.

Landowski, N., J. Tong, Joseph A. Allen, and Steven G. Rogelberg. 2019. "Effective meetings, engaged employees, and performance: meeting size matters." Society for Industrial and Organizational Psychology Conference, Bethesda, Maryland.

Mackay, Michael M., Joseph A. Allen, and Ronald S. Landis. 2017. "Investigating the incremental validity of employee engagement in the prediction of employee effectiveness: a meta-analytic path analysis." *Human Resource Management Review* 27 (1): 108–120.

Meyer, Erin. 2019. "Coversational silence." Global Leadership Network. https://globalleadership.org/videos/leading-others/conversational-silence-2.

Mroz, Joseph E., Joseph A. Allen, Dana C. Verhoeven, and Marissa L. Shuffler. 2018. "Do we really need another meeting? The science of workplace meetings." *Current Directions in Psychological Science* 27 (6): 484–491.

Singer, Jerome L., and Peter Salovey. 1991. "Organized knowledge structures and personality: Person schemas, self schemas, prototypes, and scripts." In M. J. Horowitz (Ed.), *The John D. and Catherine T. MacArthur Foundation series on mental health and development. Person schemas and maladaptive interpersonal patterns.* 33–79. University of Chicago Press.

van Eerde, Wendelien, and Sana Azar. 2020. "Too late? What do you mean? Cultural norms regarding lateness for meetings and appointments." *Cross-Cultural Research* 54 (2–3): 111–129.

Chapter 9

Remembering Virtual Meeting Etiquette

The Converged Perspective

P rior to the pandemic, video interviews – sometimes called "digital interviews" – were becoming more and more commonplace, but when COVID-19 hit, they became the *only* kind of interview. Karin shares this story from one of her clients.

A Story from Karin's Perspective

Emily had waited for this moment. Having lost her job early on as a result of cutbacks made in response to COVID-19, she was one of millions who found themselves unemployed. In the past, she would have worked her network, set up lunches with former colleagues, and attended Chamber of Commerce events to refresh old connections and create new ones, but her efforts to find a new position were stunted by a hiring landscape that was entirely remote. So, when she finally landed a promising video interview, she knew how big it was and prepared accordingly. She was ready.

When she entered the virtual meeting, though, she was met with an unusual sight. Instead of seeing the face of the interviewer reflected back in the screen, she instead saw mostly the top of his head, which was tilted to the left. He did address her when she popped into the virtual room, but the most that she saw of his face was his profile. The awkwardness deepened as he worked his way through what seemed to be a prescribed list of questions that she answered with aplomb. However, her confidence waned as her interviewer continued to look off camera, seemingly fixated on something on his desk or maybe even the floor. As her interview drew to a close, she finally did see his face in full when he glanced up to offer a few words. "Thanks. We'll be in touch." Emily's heart sank.

Lo and behold, an email hit her inbox a few hours later, offering her the position. What should have been met with total elation was actually met with a substantial dose of confusion. From Emily's point of view, the interview went terribly. She was glad she misjudged her experience, but later on, she sought clarity from her former interviewer and now boss when she relayed how she felt during the meeting. It turned out what she read as disinterest was actually a visual representation of someone paying close attention to every word she said. You see, unbeknownst to Emily, her boss was actually taking copious notes. He liked what he heard, so he wanted to make sure he captured it accurately. However, he never took the time to explain why he was looking down almost the entire time. The result? Two very different views, literally and figuratively, of how the interview went.

Neuroscience and psychology has found that it is not uncommon for two people who shared an experience to have wildly different memories of the event (Matthews 2019). We find this humorous when a husband and wife have greatly differing memories of how they met, their first kiss, or their favorite restaurant experience, and so on. We find this less humorous and more alarming when we see it in accounts of crimes or other incidents. But, we find it *everywhere*, including in the example of Emily and her boss. Two people sharing an experience together with very different memories of the event. One encoded a disinterested and disengaged interviewer, and the other encoded an enthralling interviewee with amazing answers to scripted questions.

We all have blind spots when it comes to professional etiquette in a remote meeting. It's full of nuance, and when not understood and followed, it can dramatically inhibit our ability to be effective virtually.

In this chapter, we will explore:

- The disconnect between our real-world environment and the expectations of our online audience.
- Why you may want to embrace moments of unexpected authenticity.
- Avoiding auditory interference that is within your control.
- The importance of doing a tech check.
- How a host can better ensure meeting success.

In a virtual meeting, the mistakes we make are often a result of a lack of self-awareness rather than purposeful action, but those missteps can have consequences that get in the way of our business success. You are likely very familiar with what is appropriate and what is not appropriate if you are meeting with someone face to face, but most of us are not well-versed in virtual video meeting etiquette. In the following pages, we will highlight some of the challenges you may encounter and how you can overcome them.

Business Mode from the Spare Bedroom

When corporate offices closed down, millions were sent home to cobble together their own version of a work-from-home space. The lucky ones had home offices ready to go. The *really* lucky ones had home offices with doors that they could close to keep the chaos out. However, many folks were forced to find a place to continue doing their work as unimpeded as possible. People were taking their virtual meetings from living room couches, kitchen bar stools, or even atop guest beds with throw pillows galore. Our surroundings can affect our actions, and when we are working from the comforts of our own homes, that more relaxed environment can lead to a relaxation of our level of professionalism. The bottom line, though, is when you are meeting virtually with someone, you are still in the same room with that person – albeit one that does not have physical walls. But that does not give you license to loosen up to the point of being outside the professional norms. The same rules apply as if you'd be meeting in person.

In order to reflect them, you need to ask yourself, "What are my audience's expectations of me?" How you answer this question is largely dependent upon the norms for your industry and role. For example, if you are a software engineer in Silicon Valley, showing up to an in-person meeting in a three-piece suit would garner a lot of odd looks and likely much scorn. If you walk into a meeting on Wall Street in shorts and flip-flops, you are liable to be thrown out on your ear. The work-from-home environment has bred a slight relaxation in some wardrobe norms. The most common approach falls in the "business casual" category, with the emphasis on "business" or "casual" shifting based upon the culture of the company. The exception is if you want to come across as an expert. In that case, you want to lean toward "business formal" to ensure your appearance reflects your expertise. However, audience expectations go well beyond your wardrobe. The way you conduct yourself is far more important and where we sometimes fall short.

This can manifest in many ways. Maybe you find yourself rocking back in that cushy office chair that you purchased to make your home office more comfortable. Would you lean back 45 degrees in your seat if you were sitting across the table from a potential client? Maybe you decide it is perfectly fine to slurp your leftover lo mein from last night's Chinese takeout while chatting with your team. No matter how polite you try to be, you can't possibly pull that off without grossing out those who are watching you partake.

We let down our guard when we don't have people in the physical room with us because we don't have those accountability partners to remind us what is appropriate and what is not. If we took a glance around a conference room table and realized we were the only ones lounging in our seats, we would likely sit up straight. If no one else was munching on lunch, we would probably opt to wait until after the meeting to eat. Without people in our physical spaces, we need to self-monitor our behavior and assess how it might be perceived by others who are with us on that virtual meeting. We need to constantly consider how our actions are being read by others on the other side of the lens, something that becomes harder to do when entering hour six of the day's video calls.

How can you combat this lack of self-awareness? First, start with this: give yourself an opportunity to reset between each meeting, even if it's just a five-minute stretch break. Next, use that time to determine what the audience expectations will likely be before hopping onto the next call. Finally, kick off that meeting with the right mental mindset and approach that is appropriate for whomever is joining you on the screen. As previously mentioned, even after a good meeting, you need time to cognitively switch to the next thing, and if it's another meeting, then considering whom you're meeting with, their expectations, and so forth for professional etiquette can mean the difference between a polite noncommittal meeting and a successful sales meeting.

Professional Doesn't Mean Sterile

For remote workers, finding the right balance between being professional and being authentic is one of the keys to virtual meeting success. As mentioned in Chapter 5, interruptions are inevitable and should be handled efficiently in order to get back down to business. But some of those interruptions might actually be of service to you as you seek to build rapport and deepen relationships.

One of Karin's clients experienced that during a customer call when her six-year-old daughter ran into her office unannounced and climbed up on her lap smack dab in the middle of her meeting with a key opinion leader. At first, her client was horrified, which was likely advertised on her face. To her relief, though, her conversation partner started to laugh, greeted the young interloper, and proceeded to tell a similar tale of her son who barged into one of her meetings. Rather than derailing the conversation, this "moment of unexpected authenticity" forged a bond between these two working moms that helped to build a stronger foundation for their business relationship that would likely pay dividends for months – if not years – to come.

Social psychology confirms that simple sharing of personal information can truly make for a bond that is lasting. Specifically, similarity breeds liking (Amodio and Showers 2005). When people interact and find common ground, interests, or life experiences, those similarities lead them to like each other more. Often this is used to explain the idea that "birds of a feather flock together" or that people who decide to start a relationship usually do so due to some common bond. In meetings, finding even small similarities can change the dynamic of the meeting, soften the situation, and make for a more positive inter-action, just as Karin's client learned.

Social connections matter in our personal and professional lives, and COVID-19 has blended those in such a way that there is more overlap than ever before. Opportunity knocks in unexpected ways – like a child who doesn't remember to knock before making a cameo on your video meeting. It's up to you to recognize when to embrace them and when to politely usher them out.

Keep the Pings, Dings, and Whooshes to Yourself

While a visit from a little one might be a welcome respite, no one appreciates hearing the unmistakable sound of a notification breaking into the conversation. The incessant sound effects on our phones, our laptops, our desktops, our tablets are designed to draw our attention to something other than what we are doing at that moment. However, those noises give our conversation partners the sense that we are not fully focused on them.

Have you ever been speaking to someone at a party or networking event who keeps glancing over your shoulder to see who else might be coming within orbit? It makes you feel like you are worth their time only until something else or someone else of higher value comes along. Those notifications are a signal to your meeting attendees that you are willing to turn your attention away from them if something more important demands it. It feels rude. At a minimum, turn off the audible aspect of the notification, so it's not so obvious to your audience. If they hear that *ding* and you glance down to see the cause, you have given the impression that you are not all that invested in the conversation at hand. *Ouch*.

Be Mute Savvy

As discussed briefly in Chapter 4, professional virtual etiquette around muting is clear. If you are not going to be asked to speak for a prolonged period of time, placing yourself on mute is the responsible thing to do. In fact, many platforms allow you to enter meetings on mute by default, so you have to go out of your way to unmute yourself. However, if you are participating in what is designed to be a dynamic discussion with a lot of back-and-forth dialogue, you may want to keep yourself unmuted to make it easier to engage in conversation.

Some platforms have created another capability that falls between the mute or unmute options. For example, Zoom has enabled the space bar to be almost like an intercom system. If you have yourself on mute, you can hold down the space bar to temporarily unmute yourself, which can make for a more natural entry into the discussion.

For larger meetings where the *Brady Bunch* boxes extend beyond one screen, hosts have a higher calling to take matters into their own hands and take care of renegade participants who haven't muted themselves appropriately. Most platforms give hosts the option of muting all participants in one fell swoop. It's a powerful tool that should be exercised if the experience for the majority is being compromised by the few who have failed to silence their audio.

Check Your Tech in Advance

Technology can be a fickle thing and does not always act the same way every time you go into a virtual meeting. That's why it is essential that you log in prior to the actual meeting start time to ensure your video and audio settings are up to snuff. Almost every platform has a way to assess your video output as well as the volume levels of your speakers and microphone before entering the virtual meeting room.

As with all software, updates are inevitable, and sometimes they can impact the way your hardware interacts with the platform. For example, Karin spends countless hours teaching using a certain video collaboration platform. However, one day, her webcam did not show up in the list of camera options despite her best efforts to troubleshoot. As any good tech support person would counsel, she ended up taking the nuclear option and restarted her computer. When she tried logging in again, her webcam was speaking to the platform once again and all was right with her virtual video world.

Don't waste the time of your fellow participants by spending the first five minutes of your meeting time trying to troubleshoot the tech.

You should not have to ask your audience if they can see you or hear you. You should know that you are in good shape before entering the room. If you do this in advance, it gives you time to identify a potential problem (like a webcam out of commission for no good reason) and fix it without appearing unprofessional or inconveniencing your audience.

Being the Best Host

The organizer of a meeting has a heavy influence over a meeting's success. Not only does that person have an opportunity to put settings in place that can preserve the integrity of the meeting, but he or she can also set the tone for the meeting itself through some best practices.

Keep Invaders Out

In the early days of the move to remote, so-called "Zoom bombing" became too frequent of an occurrence. Business meetings set up without privacy precautions in place were being rudely interrupted by uninvited attendees who would at a minimum be disruptive and at worst share pornographic and other offensive material without permission. The majority of the problem stemmed from oversharing of links on social media, which allowed anyone to hop into many public meetings and hijack them before the host had a chance to respond.

Since then, all of the platforms have put safeguards in place or beefed up preexisting precautions to keep people out who should not be there in the first place. However, you as a host need to make sure you have put all of the privacy options into practice, whether it be requiring passcodes to enter the meeting or instigating the use of waiting rooms so only the host can decide who gets in and who stays out. To avoid having anything shared that definitely should not be shared, adjust your settings so that only you can control who can share their screens during the meeting.

Allow for Unstructured Opportunities to Engage

Imagine you and your team are planning to meet in person for your quarterly business review. The meeting is scheduled to start at 10 a.m. and will be held in a big conference room with seating for all 12 of you. As the organizer, you like to get there ahead of time to set up the space. Plus, you know that Sheri likes to arrive early and you would like to use that time to catch up on her daughter's college search. Those opportunities to chitchat with coworkers are harder to come by in a virtual world, but are worth pursuing regardless.

Meeting science shows that those informal conversations actually lead to better business outcomes. As mentioned in Chapter 3, pre-meeting talk is a useful way to set the tone for a successful meeting. In a study of working adults from across the United States, Joe looked at four different types of pre-meeting talk (Allen, Lehmann-Willenbrock, and Landowski 2014). These included work talk (i.e. conversations used to actually engage in work), meeting preparatory talk (i.e. talking about the upcoming meeting), shop talk (i.e. talking about work-related things), and small talk (i.e. talking about the weather, TV, sports, etc.). Although all of these types of talk happen before meetings, the only one that actually relates to overall meeting effectiveness is small talk. That's right, shooting the breeze with your colleagues, even just for a minute or two before diving into work talk, can make for a better meeting.

It's up to you as the meeting host to allow for small talk to happen in a remote world. How? By creating time for it in the virtual space. As the organizer, consider opening the call early to allow people to come to the meeting on their own time. For an in-person meeting, not everyone busts through the door at one time, but it sometimes feels that way if you open the meeting room at the published start time. It can feel quite abrupt and can result in some awkward moments as you dive quickly into the agenda. If you open the call in advance, it gives you the opportunity to greet people individually as they enter the room just as you would in person. Plus, it allows others on the call to interact informally before the structured part of the meeting begins. You can then build on that easy flow of conversation by kicking off the meeting with a prompt, perhaps culled from some of the pre-meeting small talk. "So, Laura, it sounds like you had an interesting 24 hours with your dog who literally ate your homework. Want to share?"

How you end a meeting also matters. If you are the host and you close the meeting for all too soon, it can feel like you have thrown everyone outside of the room and slammed the door. It can be downright rude. If you organized the call, be the last to leave. It also allows you to mimic another in-person meeting behavior. Once a meeting adjourns, most people will leave the room, but there may be one or two who linger. Perhaps they have something they wanted to address that they did not want to bring up in front of the entire group? Create that opportunity in the virtual space for them to stay after the session to speak with you about it one-on-one.

Case Study: Professional Etiquette for the Classroom and the Clinic

When the reality of the pandemic began to sink in during those fast-moving days in mid-March, the Physician Assistant Education Association (PAEA) pivoted on a dime to respond. The mission of PAEA is to provide professional development for PA (Physician Assistant) educators at hundreds of academic institutions across the country. PAEA knew COVID-19 meant a paradigm shift for their faculty, who, like educators at all levels, were forced to move their classroom online with lightning speed.

According to Karen Hills, the chief of education development at PAEA, "Our CEO recognized very early on that we were going to have to make a really big shift. I remember getting an email on Saturday, March 7th asking me to design a webinar and collate materials for the Digital Learning Hub on best practices teaching virtually for our membership."

Hills and her colleague, Christine Vucinich, an instructional specialist, got to work immediately. In order to support their educators, they knew they needed to offer guidance in two key areas: learning strategies for online delivery and best practices for on-camera presence. Their plan based on the data from PAEA's Curriculum Report was on their CEO's desk three days later.

Like educators across the board, PA faculty had to quickly convert to videoconferencing platforms. Adjusting the pedagogy was a monumental task in and of itself, but one of the more vexing challenges was understanding how to navigate communicating the curriculum through the camera.

Within weeks, PAEA began offering a series of workshops focused on professional virtual video etiquette – touching on everything from lighting to engagement techniques. Even for the most seasoned educators, this kind of training was a saving grace as they scrambled to make the change to virtual. Hills recalls one text that came in from a long-time faculty member who had just finished the training. "That was the most helpful thing. Now I feel like I can focus on the content because I have some of the mechanics so nothing will be distracting or detracting from my objectives."

With the explosion of telehealth, PAEA also recognized a dual purpose for training on professional video etiquette. According to a survey by Sermo, an online physician network, 85% of physicians have adopted telehealth often in the form of video visits with patients, and 60% say they'll continue to use telehealth post-pandemic (Wicklund 2020). Suddenly, the curriculum for PA students needed to include a more robust on-camera presence component. According to Hills, "Part of the PA education curriculum includes that professionalism component about how you show up in the clinic, but if the clinic space is a virtual one, you have to cover some of those professionalism topics as well." So, PAEA invited students to attend virtual video training similar to the workshops offered to faculty; however, the student focus was not only on how they should show up in class but also on how they should conduct themselves in a virtual clinic setting.

Ironically, PAEA had already been exploring ways to virtualize their own offerings back in the fall of 2019. The majority of their events had historically been held in person, but that limited their reach to those who were able to attend on-site. That initiative was put on the back burner until the pandemic pushed the timeline.

"It became very immediate. Something that we had on our roadmap became moved to the forefront very quickly where we might have rolled it out in a year or maybe six months," said Vucinich. After the initial training, she has been helping to craft a litany of offerings that harness the power of virtual meetings, which allows for more frequent and immediate collaboration, regardless of geography.

"One of the things we are doing in 2021 is a virtual road trip around the country, meeting with different programs virtually to discuss thematic topics and make connections and facilitate collaboration between the programs," says Vucinich. It also allows faculty to present to others nationally, which is critical for advancement in academics.

However, PAEA learned a lot during those early days of training up faculty and students. Hills observed, "Some people may not be as comfortable sharing their slides. Some people may not know how to use a video in this virtual space. Some people may not have rehearsed how they are handing off from one slide to the next." Lesson number one: not all are innately aware of proper video etiquette. That's why practice sessions are considered a necessity to ensure the speaker's on-camera presence reflects the level of professionalism they would want to project.

Conclusion

With people spending more time than ever videoconferencing, it can be easy to forget that we are always on camera. YouTube and other media channels are rife with comical clips from folks who had forgotten that all-important fact and wound up revealing more than they wanted to in front of coworkers or customers. (No, taking your laptop into the bathroom is *not* okay.) The key is reminding yourself of the other people in the room with you and making sure your behavior reflects their presence. But how you "show up" in a virtual meeting isn't just a matter of demonstrating good virtual etiquette; it's also important to pay attention to your production value. In Chapter 10, we discuss ways to maximize how you show up, literally, on your webcam.

Chapter Takeaways

- Treat a virtual meeting as if you were meeting in the same room, because in essence you are.
- Don't sterilize your work-from-home situation. Embrace moments of unexpected authenticity.
- Silence notifications on all devices.
- Know when and how to mute and unmute yourself.

- Check your tech in advance.
- Be a good host – protect the privacy of the meeting and create space for unstructured engagement.

References

Allen, Joseph A., Nale Lehmann-Willenbrock, and Nicole Landowski. 2014. "Linking pre-meeting communication to meeting effectiveness." *Journal of Managerial Psychology* 29 (8): 1064–1081.

Amodio, David M., and Carolin J. Showers. 2005. "'Similarity breeds liking' revisited: The moderating role of commitment." *Journal of Social and Personal Relationships* 22 (6): 817–836.

Matthews, Julian. 2019. "Why two people see the same thing but have different memories." *Neuroscience News*. https://neurosciencenews.com/same-event-different-memory-10405/.

Wicklund, Eric. 2020. "COVID-19 gives providers a blueprint for new telehealth strategies." *mHealth Intelligence*. https://mhealthintelligence.com/features/covid-19-gives-providers-a-blueprint-for-new-telehealth-strategies.

Chapter 10

Ignoring the Importance of Production Value

The Converged Perspective

U sing video in a virtual meeting can provide a porthole to your home for all to see, but too often that view consists of a slice of someone's forehead and a ceiling fan whirling around. You might be thinking, "Has she even looked at her box on the screen?" Or perhaps you are thinking, "What's wrong with just showing your forehead and your ceiling fan?"

Paying proper attention to your production value – the way you look and sound to others on the call – isn't just a matter of vanity. It's about removing any distractions that might detract from your message. And a whirling ceiling fan is *very* distracting, without a doubt.

When Karin worked in TV news, she had a whole slew of people who made sure she looked and sounded her best. They fixed her lighting, adjusted her audio, and built backdrops and sets that look perfect on camera. However, now all of us are our own production crew – minus the professional expertise.

While you may not have the top-of-the-line equipment or the training of an expert video production crew, you can make small tweaks that can have a big impact on how you come across with either minimal or no financial investment.

In this chapter, we will explore:

- The role of science in virtual meeting design.
- How to choose the best background.
- The importance of lighting and how to leverage what you likely have in your environment.
- How to position your camera and yourself in the frame.
- Ways to assess your audio quality.

Meeting Science and Design Characteristics

We mentioned only briefly in Chapter 3 the importance of meeting design characteristics. Back when most meetings were face-to-face, meeting design was evaluated very differently. Typically, this refers to the conference room, the table shape/size, the chairs, the lighting, the temperature, and so on. In one of Joe's studies with his advisor, Steven Rogelberg, they looked at a variety of meeting design characteristics to discover how they related to meeting quality (Cohen et al. 2011).

The study included all of the following design characteristics:

1. Agreement Use – were ground rules set for the meeting?
2. Break Use – did the meeting include a break (useful for long meetings)?
3. Ending Promptness – did the meeting end on time"
4. Facilitator Use – was a facilitator used?
5. Agenda Accessibility – did people see the agenda *before* the meeting?
6. Length of Meeting – how long was the meeting (shorter is usually better)?

7. Lighting Quality – can you see your neighbor (i.e., was there adequate lighting in the room)?

8. Meeting Space – did the room have adequate space for the meeting?

9. Meeting Modality – was the meeting in-person, conference call, video, etc.?

10. Minutes Taken – did someone keep minutes?

11. Noise Level – was it a noisy environment for the meeting?

12. Number of Attendees – how many people were in the meeting (smaller is often better)?

13. Record of the Meeting – was the meeting recorded?

14. Refreshments – were drinks, snacks, or other food provided?

15. Seating Arrangement – were there assigned seats?

16. Starting Promptness – did the meeting start on time?

17. Temperature Comfort – was the room a comfortable temperature?

18. Attendee as Facilitator – was the facilitator an attendee of the meeting?

They measured all of these design characteristics across more than 300 meetings and then related the measures to the quality of the meeting. Of all these factors, the design characteristics that mattered most were agreement use, ending promptness, agenda accessibility, lighting quality, meeting space, refreshments, starting promptness, temperature comfort, and attendee as facilitator. Reflecting on this list, it's remarkable to think about how many of these pre–COVID-19 meeting design characteristics are still readily present in our virtual environment. As this chapter unfolds, it will become clear that just setting up a shared conference room is no longer enough. That shared conference room now includes our home office, kitchen table, guest bedroom, or wherever we might find ourselves.

Select the Right "Set" – Which Likely Is a *Real* One

By now we've all likely seen the virtual backgrounds that allow our fellow meeting participants to place themselves in all manner of locales – a beach with palm trees blowing in the breeze, in the cosmos where we appear to be floating in outer space, or even near the North Pole with a clear view of the Aurora Borealis.

But as tempted as you may be to eliminate the mess in the scene behind you by using artificial intelligence to wallpaper your background, you may be doing yourself a disservice. According to a spring 2020 survey done by Quantified Communications, a data and behavioral analytics–based communications firm, the majority of people prefer to see your actual room behind you, especially if you want to be perceived as trustworthy or authentic. The second-most popular background option? A solid-color wall. Those computer-generated virtual backgrounds trailed at a distant third (Zandan and Lynch 2020).

The danger with real sets is that they can be *too* real and reveal more about us than we want them to. Joe has a humorous and cautionary tale related to this issue.

A Story from Joe's Perspective

As part of my work, I engage in grant writing and collaborations with other institutions. One of those institutions, the FIRST Center at Drexel University, trains students to use data to help advance the safety, well-being, and performance of firefighters and other first responders. As an affiliate faculty to the FIRST Center, I often get the opportunity to interact with the students. However, since I'm headquartered at the University of Utah, and traveling to Philly for a meeting with students is costly – not to mention somewhat impossible during a pandemic – I often would take these meetings in my office.

My office has a lot of bookshelves. In fact, my properly framed and manicured background now is essentially a headshot with my shelves of books. However, before working with Karin and a production team at the University of Utah for all my video lectures, the books on my shelves were not organized so that my most professional books were behind me. Right now, you'd see things like The Cambridge Handbook of Meeting Science *or* Taking the Measure of Work *and similar useful organizational psychology titles.*

During one of my meetings with the students at the FIRST Center before I made these changes, I had a great time talking with them about organizational psychology, how I got started studying firefighters, and how to prepare for their futures as researchers or consultants or whatever. I even talked with them about the "Imposter Syndrome," a commonly experienced feeling that you're the dumbest person in the room and you don't belong there, and sometime soon, everyone's going to figure it out and call you a fraud, and so forth (Mullangi and Jagsi 2019). All great things for young budding scientists to be aware of.

A few weeks after discussing imposter syndrome, I was on another call with the managing director and the research manager for the FIRST Center, and I asked what the students thought of the session. After sharing some kind, glowing reviews, they then said that there was one problem or something I might want to consider. They said that right after the call, all the students looked at each other and one of the students said, "Was it just me, or did Dr. Allen have the Twilight Saga *books on the shelf behind him?" They all started laughing and talking about whether or not they thought I'd read them, and so on.*

To this day, I do not know if they remember the importance of having self-confidence, overcoming that imposter syndrome, and how important they are to the future of the science of safety in the fire service. But I'm guessing they remember I like Twilight *by Stephanie Meyer.*

Take Joe's word for it – you need to carefully curate what is behind you because there is no doubt everyone will be staring at it. With that in mind, here are some basics to consider as you select your set:

Conduct a Home Edit

This is no time to break into a sweat. The home edit is only necessary for a very small slice of your location seen through the camera lens. You can have a mess of catastrophic proportions on either side of you as long as it's out of the shot, but the view right behind you needs to be uncluttered. Why? You don't want anything to pull focus from you, the speaker.

What do people *really* want to see in your *real* background? That question was posed during that same survey conducted by Quantified Communications, which found that 44% of survey respondents preferred a wall with books or bookshelves and 34% would like to see wall art, diplomas, or photographs (Zandan and Lynch 2020). However, that still leaves quite a bit of room for interpretation. A bookshelf chock full of tchotchkes would likely not do you any favors. The same would be true for a collage of photos taking up the majority of the wall behind you.

Assume your position on the screen and take a close look at what your viewers will be able to see behind you. If your eye is drawn to something, you can be sure the eyes of your audience will be as well. Remove it unless you think it might be a conversation starter. A prized autographed baseball in a decorative glass cube could catch the eye of a fellow fan, which would allow you to develop a better business relationship through a common love of the game. However, one conversation starter is fine. Ten are not.

What Good Looks Like

The reliance on video in virtual meetings spawned an unusual business: the interior designing of "Zoom" rooms. Residents Understood, a Washington, D.C., design firm, developed a virtual design offering for clients who are hoping for some professional expertise in setting up their broadcast space, with packages ranging from a video tour of your home followed by a checklist of ways to make it camera-ready to a more expansive one with a full design plan and an individualized Pinterest board of products and ideas (Kashino 2020).

However, the DIY approach can also pay off bigtime. One of Karin's clients took her coaching tips to heart and transformed her home office into something straight out of HGTV. Using pictures and knickknacks she had around her house, she was able to beautify her bookshelf and create a pleasing but non-distracting backdrop for her video meetings.

Courtesy: Catherine Thorson

Ignoring the Importance of Production Value

Don't Sterilize Your Set

Barring a bookshelf or a gallery wall, you may go to the other end of the spectrum and opt for a blank wall. While it fits the category of "uncluttered," it feels impersonal to your audience. Plus, if you situate yourself smack up against it, you can appear to be having your driver's license picture taken.

If you don't have any other option, at least try to create some depth. Make sure there is space between you and the wall behind you. Several feet will add a bit of dimension to your shot. One quick fix for the stark wall could be a small table with a houseplant to the right or left of you to soften the image.

When to Opt for a Virtual Background

There may be situations where your real set is simply *too* real, and a virtual background may make sense. Say you're sharing a space with three roommates who are all working from home out of your tight quarters. If it's a high probability that one or two of those folks will walk behind you during a video meeting, you may want to consider throwing up that virtual background.

Make sure you take these factors into consideration:

- Your virtual background should still reflect the level of professionalism that would be expected of you. Many companies have created approved virtual backgrounds that are branded and can provide standardization for remote workers. Check with your company to see what options they offer and follow their guidelines.

- Check the tech in advance before using it during a high-stakes meeting. Yes, the artificial intelligence used to layer them over the image is pretty impressive, but it's not perfect. We have all seen the fuzzy edges where the person ends and the background begins or body parts that are eaten by the AI. Karin had a client attempt to use a virtual background, but instead of it becoming her backdrop, it became her face. The only way you could make out that it was a person was that her glasses were still visible over the bright green grass that had replaced her facial features.

- The more uniform the canvas, the easier it will be for the virtual background to layer smoothly. If you are sitting in front of a blank wall, the artificial intelligence can more easily read where you end and the background begins. The likely result is crisp edges minus the fuzziness that screams "fake."

For most people, the virtual backgrounds are more novelty than utility but can be used as an icebreaker when meted out judiciously. One of Karin's clients leverages them as icebreakers for initial sales training, now being delivered remotely. Each day, new employees are asked to pick a different picture to impose as their backgrounds based upon a theme like "Your Favorite Vacation Spot" (Who knew Angela can't get enough of whitewater rafting?) or "Your Favorite Movie" ("May the Force be with you, too!"). Every day offers a little more insight into their coworkers' interests and personalities, helping to create connections and develop rapport virtually.

Case Study: Fake a Zoom Meeting?

No doubt, sometimes trying to appear engaged and interested through what may be your fifth or sixth Zoom meeting of the day can feel exhausting.

While many of us lamented our Zoom fatigue, it inspired one creative genius (or villain, depending upon our point of view) to innovate a life hack to at least temporarily free oneself from the shackles of never-ending video calls. Enter Brian White, an entre-preneur and YouTuber, who posts all manner of online video production tips and tricks on his channel VideoZeus. His post on April 21, 2020, found a rapt audience for his video tutorial, "How to FAKE a Zoom Meeting – Clone Yourself on Video."

Over the course of a few minutes, Brian teaches us how to fool our fellow meeting participants by using a previously recorded video of ourselves as a virtual background – without ourselves in the foreground or *anywhere* in the frame (White 2020).

It does take some work to take the "work" out of the meeting itself, but in a few simple steps, Brian explains the process of making your own "virtual reality" you. It begins with recording your own Zoom meeting where you are the only attendee. Once you hit record, Brian offers these directorial tips: "What I'd suggest you do is perk up. Look normal. Look at the camera, be making eye contact with the camera." After about 30–50 seconds, you can stop the recording, download the video file, and apply the finishing touches. With some quick edits, you can create a virtual meeting "clone" of yourself where you are always on your best behavior.

Creative? Absolutely. Foolproof? Not necessarily . . . and probably a very risky proposition. Brian even admitted that when he tested it out, he was caught slipping back into the frame by the meeting organizer. When questioned about the oddity, Brian attributed it to a "glitch" in the software.

From a quick scan of the comments section, it appears that this is an appealing option for many students who find hope in the boredom of online school. But as many also pointed out, what happens when the teacher asks the "fake you" a question?

Control the Lighting

One of the most important aspects of your production value is the easiest to fix, your lighting. Remember that the best way to build trust and believability is through eye contact, but if your eyes are obscured in shadow, you miss out on the opportunity. With that in mind, here are some do's and don'ts to ensure you are seen in the best light possible.

Windows Can Be Your Friend or Your Enemy

When selecting your set, you may have been drawn to that lovely view out your window. Surely you would want to share that with your fellow meeting attendees. Unfortunately, if you place yourself in front of that big picture window, the only thing your audience will likely see is you in silhouette and an overly exposed blast of light. Backlighting is bad, plain and simple, so that window that you figured would be a perfect backdrop is actually one of the worst. However, that window may be your best asset in your space, provided that you reorient yourself to face it.

Natural light is the easiest to harness and often the most flattering. If you face a window, you will be lit evenly and smoothly. This might require some redecorating of your space, but relocating your desk to a spot that allows you to capture that soft light coming in can be much less of a hassle than troubleshooting artificial lighting options. One caveat, though: if you have a window where the sun streams in, your camera will not be able to handle that kind of shine. It'll be too harsh on your face and throw off the color balance within the rest of the frame. In that case, you may need to pull the blinds and create a lighting setup that works in that space.

Overhead Lights Are Not Enough

Flipping the wall switch and turning on your ceiling lights may seem like a no-muss, no-fuss option, but relying upon overhead lights alone is a mistake. Downward-directed light will usually result in you appearing to have raccoon eyes or dark circles. It will not be flattering and will also impede your ability to make eye contact with your audience. Instead, focus on front lighting.

Grab a lamp or two and place them in front of you. If your environment allows it, place a lamp directly behind your webcam. If that's not possible, make sure you use two lights that you can place on either side of your setup. If you only use one lamp, you will likely leave one side in shadow.

A quick web search will also reveal a plethora of lighting options that work well for video meetings. Some of them clip directly onto your laptop, but beware that the rechargeable battery–operated ones will typically dim rather quickly, which means that you could go dark with little warning on a longer call. Ring lights, made popular by YouTubers and other social media mavens, come in a wide variety of sizes and price points. Some of them plug into a wall while others have a USB connection for power.

Whether you purchase a light solely for the purpose of video calls or you leverage what you already have on hand, remember good lighting is all about balance. Take note of what lighting sources you have within your space. If you have a window to your right, that means you'll want to balance out that natural light by placing an artificial light on your left.

The light in your space might also change throughout the day depending upon the orientation of your room where you are conducting the meetings. Morning calls might be lit well, but by 4 p.m., that afternoon sun might be blasting through your space. Make sure you have ways to tweak your lighting to adjust for the variations.

Glare on Your Glasses

For those of us who wear glasses, lighting presents another challenge of keeping glare off of your lenses. You've likely seen the computer screen of your colleague reflected back at you, or even the circle from the ring light that he or she dutifully bought to improve their production value, all for naught.

You may be tempted to keep your glasses off during calls to eliminate the problem, but if you need them to clearly see your screen to read notes or slides, then you absolutely should wear them. However, there are some tricks you can try to minimize the glare:

- Place your light above your head and to the side. Think about pictures you've seen from movie or TV sets. They usually have giant box lights on tall stands. Obviously, you don't need to invest in professional-grade lighting, but you can certainly use the technique of raising your light source. If you have your light right beside your webcam, the light will be reflected directly back at you and consequently will show directly in your lenses. Raising it changes the angle of reflection so you can actually see your eyeballs.

- Consider adding more ambient lighting in your space, so the light above your head isn't the sole source. As long as you have decent front lighting, you can add dimension to your room by turning on some other lights in your space. Even feel free to flick on those overhead lights, provided that they are not your only source of light in the room.

- Use diffused light if possible. A shade will diffuse the light and reduce any shadows that might result if you simply pointed the bare bulb of a desk lamp at your face.

- Using a window for your light source and getting glare? Set yourself up at a slight angle to the window. How much of an angle will depend upon the size of the window as well as your glasses.

Once your glasses are glare-free, do avoid looking at the light. Remember it's all about angles. If you direct your gaze at the light, it will show up once again in your lenses.

TRY THIS

Sometimes the best sets are the ones you don't suspect. However, there's an easy way to uncover their existence. Put your smartphone in selfie mode and move around your potential virtual video meeting location. Pivot throughout the room and take note of the changes in lighting. Look for the angle that allows you to be lit best. This process is called "finding the light."

Now take note of what's in your background. If you have a bit of clutter in the shot, remove anything that might be distracting. If your backdrop is a bit too stark, consider what you can do to add visual interest, like wall art or even a plant on a small table.

Standing in the middle of an open space for a video call won't work, so determine if your furniture setup will allow you to utilize this spot. Karin co-opted a hall table to use for her video meetings, which she conducts not from her home office but from her spare bedroom, which she has staged for that purpose. Remember, no one knows how you have created your shot. They only see what the lens shows them.

Once you've figured out an option for you, let it be plug and play. You're more likely to use best practices if you only have to grab your seat and go.

Shape Your Shot

When speaking via video on a virtual meeting, your goal is to emulate a face-to-face interaction, but knowing how to use the tools at your disposal to accomplish this may be out of sight . . . just like your chin may be if you haven't framed yourself appropriately. Allow us to share some rules that are simple to apply but are often overlooked.

Look Them in the Eye

During a sit-down meeting in person, we are typically looking at each other on the same level aside from minor differences in torso length. So why is it so common in virtual meetings for people to appear to be looking down on everyone, as if they are pontificating from on high?

With so many people using their laptops for virtual video calls, it seems only natural to keep our devices placed on our desks or wherever we have found space to set up shop. Unfortunately, this situation results in people looking down their noses at those who have joined them on a call or, even worse, allows for a look *up* their noses via the camera below.

The ideal camera position is at eye level. That means if you are sitting or standing, you want to be looking straight ahead at the lens. If your configuration doesn't automatically account for that, you will need to adjust. Say you are using a laptop camera or you have your external webcam clipped onto the top of the screen. A low-tech solution would dictate that you place that laptop on a stack of books or a box that elevates it to the right level. If you find it a bit too perilous of a perch, purchase a laptop stand that will provide a more stable base.

If you have your webcam on your monitor, often it's positioned too high, forcing you to look up at the lens. This can undercut your authority, giving an impression like you are a kid asking a parent for permission. The solution may be to pluck the webcam from the top of the monitor. Many external webcams have a universal thread for a tripod that allows you to mount them on a tripod, which can give you total control over the placement of the webcam. This can come in especially handy if you are using multiple monitors. Try placing the tripod between the monitors, so you can easily move between the content on the screen and the camera. As mentioned in Chapter 4, there are times when you want your audience to be looking at you and times when you want to direct their attention to your visual aid, be it in a demo or a slide deck. If you minimize the physical distance between the monitors and your camera, it'll be easier for you to move your gaze back and forth. If your camera is too far away from the monitor, it'll feel like too dramatic of an expanse for your head and eyes to travel.

No More Ceiling Shots

Another critical factor in shaping your shot is how your camera is angled. You want it to be pointing straight behind you and not up. If you can see your ceiling in your shot, that is a dead giveaway that your camera is not angled properly. Square it off with the wall behind you and promise yourself that you will never show the ceiling fan again. Your fellow meeting attendees will be forever grateful.

Create the Proper Head Space

With a virtual video meeting, you are already working with fewer data points to interpret body language, but you can make a challenging situation even more difficult if you remove body parts from the picture. You want to sit squarely in the frame. Don't cut off the top of your head and don't chop off your chin. Make sure your conversation partner can see you with clear margins on three sides. Leave space between the top of your head and the top of the screen but be sure to sit tall in the frame, so you occupy at least three-quarters of the frame. Center yourself creating an even amount of space on either side of your body or else you will appear lopsided, and allot at least some wiggle room on either side of your shoulders. Otherwise, your shot will appear cramped and be uncomfortable for your viewer to watch.

If you are using a smartphone or tablet, you have one more thing to keep in mind. While it might feel most natural to set your device in portrait mode, that vertical orientation could be a mismatch with how your meeting attendees are viewing you. While the number of mobile users of video collaboration platforms has increased rapidly, most people still join using their laptops or desktops. Your video will likely be seen on a horizontal screen, and if you are sitting in vertical mode, your video will likely have black bars on either side of it. Turn that phone or tablet on its side and take full advantage of all of the screen real estate.

Don't Overlook Your Audio

When we appear on a webcam, we typically cannot hear ourselves speak. Consequently, it makes it difficult to assess the quality of our audio. Sure, you can (and should) do the audio tests in advance of both your speakers and microphone, but even those pre-meeting checks can be deceiving. What sounds good to your ears may be tinny or muffled to those of your audience.

There are many options from which to choose, whether you opt for the built-in microphone on your laptop or a speakerphone pod or a headset. However, what audio option works best for you is a product of your environment and the device you are using to carry the sound. Does your space have carpet, curtains, or other materials that can absorb sound, or do you have nary a rug in sight? For example, Karin has a high-quality microphone that she uses when recording voiceovers in her home studio that is decked out with appropriate soundproofing, but when she attempts to use that same microphone in her office, the audio is echo-y. The reason? Her downtown office is very industrial with concrete floors and lots of glass. While the aesthetic is very appealing, sound bounces all over the place. The high-quality microphone had to go back to the studio, and her $20 lapel microphone, placed right below her chin, became the go-to choice.

You also need to consider the level of ambient noise you may have in your environment. Children, animals, and partners, who are also conducting meetings from the same space, can be an auditory distraction for you and your audience. A headset or headphones may be well worth the investment to allow all to stay focused on the call and business at hand.

TRY THIS

The only way you can truly assess how you sound on a call is by either asking a trusted colleague for help or recording yourself within a video meeting platform and playing back the recording. If you've asked a colleague for help, make sure they give you honest feedback on how you sound to them. Does your voice sound full? Do you sound like you are talking through a tin can? Does the traffic noise outside your window bleed through too much? If you have a couple of different audio devices (the built-in microphone, earbuds, an external microphone on a webcam), try toggling between them and asking your conversation partner what sounds best. If you are flying solo, toggle back and forth while recording yourself and make sure that you announce what device you are using each time. Then listen back to the recording and let your own ears help you judge.

The importance of good audio quality cannot be oversold. After all, without video, a meeting can still go on, albeit with less impact. However, a meeting isn't possible without audio . . . unless you are really good at miming, playing charades, or sign language.

Here's a quick checklist for you to use to ensure your production value is up to snuff.

Production Value Considerations		
Competency	Criteria	Yes or No
Framing	Presenter takes up three-quarters of the frame with adequate space above head and on either side	[ ] Yes [ ] No
Lighting	Presenter's face is well-lit from the front	[ ] Yes [ ] No
Background	Background is uncluttered, not distracting, and has some visual interest	[ ] Yes [ ] No
Camera Angle	Camera is at eye level with no ceiling in view	[ ] Yes [ ] No
Attire	Attire is appropriate and non-distracting	[ ] Yes [ ] No
Video Quality	Video quality is adequate and connection is stable	[ ] Yes [ ] No
Background Noise	No background noise distracts from the presenter	[ ] Yes [ ] No
Audio Quality	Audio quality is adequate and connection is stable	[ ] Yes [ ] No
	TOTAL YES	[ ]

Conclusion

Being mindful of how you show up for a virtual video meeting isn't a matter of vanity. It's being respectful of your fellow attendees. Your job is to remove anything that will distract from the meeting, and if people can't get past the blazing light coming from behind you or are fixated on the half of your face that is somehow hidden from view, that's a problem that impacts the overall effectiveness of the meeting itself. Sure, you may be of the mind that you *always* want to put your best face forward when joining a virtual video call, but even if you don't, you should at least consider the costs for you and for all of those who are depending upon you to be your best self no matter the modality.

Chapter Takeaways

- Curate your background so it is uncluttered and visually appealing.

- Focus on front lighting and avoid overwhelming back lighting at all costs.

- Put your camera at eye level to emulate a face-to-face interaction.

- Make sure the camera is pointing at the wall behind you and not up.

- Sit squarely in the frame.

- Assess the quality of your audio by asking a trusted colleague when on a call or recording yourself and playing it back.

References

Cohen, Melissa A., Steven G. Rogelberg, Joseph A. Allen, and Alexandra Luong. 2011. "Meeting design characteristics and attendee perceptions of staff/team meeting quality." *Group Dynamics: Theory, Research, and Practice* 15 (1): 90.

Kashino, Marisa M. 2020. "These DC interior designers are making over people's zoom rooms." *Washingtonian*. https://www.washingtonian.com/2020/06/26/these-dc-interior-designers-are-making-over-peoples-zoom-rooms/.

Mullangi, Samyukta, and Reshma Jagsi. 2019. "Imposter syndrome: Treat the cause, not the symptom." *Jama* 322 (5): 403-404.

White, Brian. 2020. "How to FAKE a Zoom meeting: Clone yourself on video." YouTube. https://www.youtube.com/watch?v=eprkLhdqh4U.

Zandan, Noah, and Hallie Lynch. 2020. "Dress for the (remote) job you want." *Harvard Business Review*. https://hbr.org/2020/06/dress-for-the-remote-job-you-want.

Chapter 11

Building Organizational Culture Through Virtual Meetings

The Converged Perspective

Have you ever heard, "Well, that's how we do it around here," or "Oh, let me show you how we do it," or "People here kind of think this way about things"? If so, then you've experienced organizational culture.

According to the Society for Human Resource Management, organizational culture is defined as the shared values and beliefs framed by organizational leaders. These values and beliefs are communicated and maintained through a variety of methods that ultimately direct employee behaviors, perceptions, and understanding of their work environment and the world in which the organization operates (SHRM 2020).

Every organization has an organizational culture that enables and constrains employee behavior. Most of the time, as employees are on-boarded, they are socialized to see things a certain way, behave a certain way, and do things a certain way (Ostroff, Kinicki, and Muhammad 2012). Organizational culture manifests in many ways, from the types of equipment and software that are used to even the choice of beverage offered in the corporate cafeteria. That's why we laugh at the commercials where a Coca-Cola delivery man drinks a Pepsi. If you're a Coke employee, any desire to drink Pepsi is socialized out of you – and should you swig a Pepsi now and then, you do so privately.

All of this is to say that just as organizations have their own "way of doing things," organizations also have a way of conducting meetings: their meeting culture. But when meetings are suddenly virtual, what happens to that meeting culture and the culture of the company writ large?

In this chapter, we explore:

- What meeting culture is and how it operates for individuals and teams.
- How to build a positive meeting culture.
- The importance of virtual meetings as businesses carry on.
- How socialization into the organizational culture starts in the meeting culture.

Meeting Culture Is a Reality

As we begin, let's be clear: meeting culture is real. However, the idea of meeting culture and the need to study it by scientists emerged rather recently. In 2015, Joe and his colleagues started by investigating how different organizations seem to be more oriented toward meetings than others. In a series of interviews with CEOs and other leaders in organizations, Joe learned that as people moved from organization to organization through their careers, they experienced a dramatically different number of meetings, time spent in meetings, and experiences in meetings. One CEO even stated, "I knew the minute I walked in the door and experienced one day of meetings that I was only going to be with that organization until I could find another place to work." What struck us about this comment was how it sprang from meetings – not culture, the people, or even the work itself – but rather, how individuals within the organization met.

That leads us to introduce the concept of meeting orientation, which we define as the degree to which an organization and its groups or teams are focused on meetings (Hansen and Allen 2015). Specifically, organizations with a high meeting orientation implicitly or explicitly encourage employees to use group and team meetings as an important form of interaction and the overall work process. Meeting orientation is about the degree or frequency with which groups and teams in the organization meet. High-meeting-orientated organizations may hold many workplace meetings while low-meeting-orientated organizations tend to hold fewer meetings. However, those group and team meetings are not necessarily good ones. Meeting orientation focuses on the number of meetings, but it's the *quality* of those meetings that determines whether a meeting culture is an advantage *or* a great hindrance to an organization's effective functioning (Mroz et al. 2019).

The term "meeting culture" started to gain traction both as a manifestation of and an enabler of organizational culture. Earlier, we defined meeting culture as the shared values and beliefs framed by organizational leaders around workplace meetings that are communicated and maintained through a variety of methods. These values direct employee behaviors, perceptions, and understanding of how they should meet within their organization. In other words, it's the *meeting specific* organizational culture. For example, Jeff Bezos is known for his "two-pizza rule," which states that no meeting should be so large that two pizzas can't feed the whole group. Whether he meant to or not, he's following sound group and team science, which indicates that for decision-making groups, five to seven people (as we mentioned in Chapter 3) is optimal for maximum participation and collaboration.

Other organizations have implemented top-down rules around meetings that start to solidify and establish their meeting culture. For example, a recent trend is for organizations to designate a "no meeting day" (Reisenwitz 2020). In this way, the organization is trying to give its employees some uninterrupted time to get their other work done. Logitech implemented a "No Meeting Friday" effort to try to do exactly that – with the stipulation that sales calls are still okay for Friday, but all internal meetings were to stop. This decision, among other things, continues to shape their meeting culture.

Organizational leaders establish both the meeting culture and overall culture of their organization through their meetings. If an organization has a set of espoused values, they might wonder if those values are actually present among their employees. In meetings, the values of the organization are on display – and we're talking about the actual values, not the ones printed on the mission statement. The behaviors enacted by the employees are a reflection of those values as they seek to fulfill the tasks set for them by leadership (Tsao 2020). Meetings are a window into the soul (or as we've called it, the culture) of an organization. You might be wondering, "What does the soul of my organization look like?" Be a fly on the wall of your organization's meetings, and you'll get an idea pretty fast.

How to Build a Positive Meeting Culture

As with all things, you can have a good meeting culture *or* a bad meeting culture. In fact, most organizations probably have an "okay" meeting culture. The reason we say that is, with more than half of all meetings being rated as poor (Mroz et al. 2018), a good amount of not-so-good behavior occurs in nearly every meeting. But, we also have enough *good* going on in meetings to keep us coming back to them as an extremely useful and flexible tool.

So, how do we build a positive meeting culture in our teams and our organization? Well, it starts with the individual. It starts with you. Remember Chapters 3,4,5,6, and what we considered the core of best practices for meetings in our suddenly virtual world? That is the starting point. We have to get back to the basics and learn the new basics. If you've read this book up to this point, you've essentially taken Meetings 101 from the meeting scientist and the on-camera coach. And we are unified in our message! Do the introspection and identify a few things you can start doing to make your meetings better. Do it, do it now, and keep on doing it.

Be an Influencer

If you are a leader, you have more influence over creating a positive meeting culture than most of your colleagues. Leaders have the opportunity to set ground rules in their groups. These rules tend to be adopted, copied, and used elsewhere. But if not, you can inspire your coworkers by how you conduct yourself even as an attendee. As you engage in good meeting behavior, you become a peer who can positively pressure others into engaging in similar behavior. You become an example of better meeting behavior.

Joe just recently planned and hosted a session for a large conference. For that meeting, he outlined a plan, set ground rules, and facilitated the session. You might think, "Yeah, sure, of course the meeting scientist does that, but how does that apply to me?" Well, when Joe set a good example of what good looks like, it was recognized. His outlined plan is now being adopted by other session leaders for that conference, and even additional conference leaders are asking for it. The point? Good ground rules and process are infectious, and as you adopt them, others will copy and implement them.

Additionally, if you are part of the leadership team, there's nothing that stops you from leading the effort to manage and develop your meeting culture by doing a meeting audit focused on change. By audit, go back to those "fly on the wall" observations we mentioned in the previous section and do them. See what meetings are really like and then map out a plan to change them. Decree a universal change in your group, division, or organization and then hold people accountable through standard means. Joe can count on one hand the number of organizations he's met that had meetings as a section on their performance evaluation tool for employees and managers.

Finally, for something to become a *shared* value, belief, or behavioral approach, it must be rewarded, supported, and encouraged. Thus, at all levels of the organization, good meeting behavior should be rewarded, supported, encouraged, and codified into standard operating procedures (SOPs). But the converse holds as well. Bad meeting behaviors should be discouraged, sanctioned, and even entered into the disciplinary action domain at all levels of the organization. For example, habitual lateness is a problem that dramatically impacts the quality of workplace meetings. You can expect a meeting that starts late to be at least 10% worse than it could have been, and more likely it becomes one of the many "poor" meetings in one's workday (Allen, Lehmann-Willenbrock, and Rogelberg 2018). If someone is consistently causing these late starts, the science would support disciplinary action. After all, from a loss protection scheme, if you knew that something caused a 10% loss of organizational performance, wouldn't that be a target for improvement? Of course it would, so it's important to allow peer pressure and effective leadership to be the hallmarks of efforts made to establish a meaningfully positive group, team, and organizational meeting culture.

Introducing New Employees to a Suddenly Virtual Organization

Up to now, this chapter has been focused on meeting culture before the seismic shift of the pandemic. Now, we must acknowledge that business has forever changed. We are suddenly virtual, engaging in remote work at rates never before seen in the history of the modern world. Businesses adapt to challenges, and needs arise for new people, new positions, and so forth. The speed of business requires flexibility and adaptation, and now we must hire, socialize, and onboard new employees in an on-camera world.

Meeting culture not only impacts our traditional meeting setting, with our teams and our leaders, but also in other important areas in the workplace from sales calls to hiring processes. After all, with most meetings required to be virtual to allow for adequate social distance, and business in some areas (e.g. IT) growing dramatically, the applicant interview now occurs in a one-on-one virtual meeting.

Video interviewing was starting to gain a foothold before COVID-19 but quickly became *the* way to hire when face-to-face meetings became off-limits. Everything we discussed in Chapters 5 and 6 about being more effective on-camera applies to both sides of this equation: the hiring organization and the potential new hire. Successful interviewing is a skill that requires effective communication, listening, and processing of information. Successful interviewees are those who are attentive, responsive to questions, appropriately inquisitive, and so on. During an interview, both the interviewer and interviewee are *on*, and right now they are also on camera. If you are currently looking for a job, the techniques discussed in those chapters are not simply good ideas to consider, but they may very well be the difference between being hired and being passed over.

In response to the switch to virtual, new resources are becoming available for hiring managers on how to hire during a pandemic (Grensing-Pophal 2020). Not only do managers need to look for a person who possesses the right traditional skills for the job, but they also have new considerations to keep in mind. Strong on-camera presence may be a top priority for those in sales who will be conducting virtual sales calls rather than meeting on site. In addition, hiring managers need to be sensitive to concerns over physical contact, colocated versus remote work, and the pace of onboarding.

Onboarding in a Virtual World

Remote onboarding is more than just a series of online trainings and a digital copy of the employee handbook. Live virtual training needs to be included in the form of spaces where people interact, have opportunities to ask questions, and more effectively absorb the necessary information. In other words, hiring managers and HR professionals need to be deliberate about how they *meet* with new hires and bring them into the organization. In fact, the onboarding process has become such a concern that a quick Web search will uncover multiple lists outlining appropriate steps for effective virtual onboarding (Indeed 2020).

For example, Indeed.com shared the following 16 steps to successful virtual onboarding, which Joe expands upon to give you a greater context. (His comments will appear in *italics*.) Please note that these are primarily for knowledge workers and workers immediately entering into remote work situations. However, the general ideas would likely still apply for workers who have on-site options or requirements.

1. Have them complete new hire paperwork

As with any new job, there's loads of paperwork to do. Everyone expects it, so keep it simple, help them use an e-signature tool, and allow them to have the familiarity of the I-9.

2. Create an agenda for the first week

Provide them a bit more structure the first week. In many cases, there will be plenty of online training and so forth to work through. Schedule check-ins and opportunities for them to ask questions. They need to feel taken care of but not over-whelmed with attention.

3. Email them a welcome message

The welcome email is often a neat way to share links to organizational resources that they need to know about. It can also serve as a polite way to start a conversation about other tasks that need to occur during that first week.

4. Deliver work equipment

New hires probably need new equipment, such as a company-provided computer, webcam, headset, and so on.

5. Send a welcome kit

A welcome kit could include a copy of the employee handbook, benefits package description/details on enrollment, and some much-needed company swag.

6. Assign a welcome buddy

As previously mentioned, remote work can be isolating. Most organizations have a mentor program. This should be adapted for an online format, so they have a "welcome buddy" or simply a mentor who can give them another, less formal contact point, both by helping to reduce feelings of isolation as well as offering an insider's insight into "how things are done around here."

7. Add them to all relevant communication channels

Make sure they are on all the appropriate email lists, calendars, and communication streams via the company intranet.

8. Inform your current team of their arrival

Inform the team of a new person's arrival and allow them to reach out to make informal connections where possible before the next team meeting. This will likely occur initially in an email or other electronic communication, and then more informal introductions should occur inside the virtual meeting.

9. Get them online as soon as possible

Obviously, the sooner they get connected, the sooner most of these steps can happen. The sooner they are online, interacting with their team and starting tasks, the better. Their own internal network at the organization won't start until their VPN allows them into the right places.

10. Meet the team (no handshakes required)

Preferably in the first week, get them in a meeting with their team (remember to introduce them first!). Let the introductions occur naturally, allow folks to discuss their functions on the team, and even consider engaging in processes to allow some casual interaction.

11. Hold company orientation

Help them get to know the company that they are now a part of. Consider what you want them to know immediately *about the company and team culture. Does that include history, organizational structure, mission/values, HR policies, etc.? This could be done with a group of new hires where fea-sible, but it's definitely an important process in an employee's onboarding/socialization.*

12. Keep onboarding interactive

Sure, face-to-face makes interaction easier, but the science is clear that interactive activities are more effective at helping people learn and retain information. To the degree possible, consider gamifying the onboarding experience, engaging in icebreakers where meaningful, and giving them multiple ways to rehearse the important information about their team.

13. Go over role responsibilities and expectations

We were surprised to learn that an Indeed survey found that 44% of new hires left their jobs within the first six months, citing unclear guidelines about their responsibilities and expectations. It stands to reason that if you hire someone to do a job, onboarding should include some pretty extensive direction on what they are supposed to be doing, goal-setting, and having check-ins related to those goals over their early tenure with the organization.

14. Schedule frequent new employee one-on-ones with their manager

Help them schedule regular meetings with their manager, so they can establish the necessary professional relationship, understand expectations, and learn how to operate effectively on their team.

15. Build in spontaneity

It might seem odd to suggest spontaneity in the onboard-ing process, but think about your own experience being brought into an organization pre-pandemic. I'm guessing members of the team went to coffee with you or rearranged their schedule to have a meet-up as a team for lunch, happy-hour, celebrate a birthday, etc. Just because we are suddenly virtual, doesn't mean we can't be spontaneous and allow for some socializing that communicates the values of the team.

16. Collect virtual onboarding feedback

It wouldn't be a good set of steps if the last step wasn't getting feedback on the process and using that feedback to adjust and improve the onboarding process. This continuous improvement perspective is truly essential when we find ourselves changing major aspects of a process due to unforeseen challenges.

Organizational Socialization Through Virtual Meetings

As wonderful as the indeed.com list is, with the important modifications and updates for the virtual meeting environment, onboarding is just the beginning. How does organizational socialization for these newcomers occur? What tools are leveraged to communicate the values and strategic aims of the organization and how they fit into them? The answer to both of these questions is once again virtual meetings.

In virtual meetings, the window to the organization's soul – those values, strategic aims, and how individuals fit (or don't fit) with the organization – will become apparent. And for now, that information will need to be communicated via employee online interactions. And the quicker that can happen, the better for the organization and the individual. Organizations do not want their people communicating or sharing inconsistent values, images, or ideas about what it means to be a member of the organization.

Thus, new kinds of meetings are needed to create opportunities for socialization into the organization, the team within the organization, and so on. Virtual socializing sessions may be needed to get a new team member acclimated to their team, build rapport, and establish expectations. In other words, welcome to the business world of pop-up "Happy Hour" or Friday "Dance Parties" – these meetings have become the location for organizational socialization.

We recommend finding the right mix of social event-like meetings for your organization. However, the right mix is not a one-size-fits-all endeavor. Remember, organizational cultures are different, so the method by which socialization to the organization occurs might look a little different across the virtual platforms. Perhaps a "dance party" for the team online would be absurd in one organization but exactly the perfect thing to do for another. Like many of our other suggestions, we recommend an experimental approach. Try some ideas out, like a five-minute warm-up to each meeting asking how folks are doing, or happy hours on Friday, or any number of other ideas. See what works for your organization and your team, and keep after it.

Case Study: #WeAreLenovo

Since 2013, the Lenovo LASR (Lenovo Accelerated Sales Rotation) program has been recruiting top university graduates who have a passion for technology and an aptitude for sales and who jump at the chance to work for one of the top information technology companies in the world. The highly competitive two-year program combines immersive sales training with rotational business and sales placements coupled with professional development opportunities. Always with an eye for the future, the program is designed to develop the leaders of tomorrow, in part by introducing them to the leaders of Lenovo today.

"LASRs are the best and brightest from their respective universities. They are our future leaders of Lenovo, and rightfully so as we onboard them it's critical we make an impact as we introduce them into our company culture," said Kori Christensen, Senior LASR Program Manager and Talent Development, Lenovo North America.

But for the class of 2020, known as Generation 10, that showcasing, that inculcation into the culture itself, would need to be done remotely.

Kori recalled those early planning days, showered in uncertainty for all: "As many businesses were pivoting to virtual onboarding and remote work for the first time, LASR was preparing to onboard 25 full-time employees and 13 summer interns. Our overall goal was to give them the same experience, but this time, through their PC. There was a level of pressure to execute flawlessly, as this was uncharted territory for everyone. However, being a global tech pioneer we had the resources and tools to effectively make it happen."

Lenovo had a distinct advantage as a tech leader in figuring out how to make "onboarding from home" work. Lenovo rallied their resources to ensure the LASRs would have the tools they needed in their hands a few days prior to their official start date by shipping their Lenovo hardware directly to their doorsteps.

Meanwhile, Lenovo's North America training team looked at ways to translate the in-person classroom experience to a virtual one delivered to their homes while maintaining the integrity of the process. The typical on-site schedule for the first two weeks is intense as LASRs are brought up to speed. However, while that schedule was kept largely intact, there was one critical change. They added a lot more breaks to account for the potential burnout that could result from long days spent sitting in front of a computer.

Another key component of those first two weeks? Building a network within Lenovo itself. Organizational leaders had already marked off their calendars to meet with the LASRs in person. While the pandemic eliminated that possibility, the training team ensured that those meetings still happened, even though they had to occur through a webcam.

"I always tell the LASRs, 'Your network is your net worth. Don't be scared to talk with all your colleagues. I know it may be intimidating to meet with a Lenovo executive on your third day in a virtual environment, but remember we're all human,'" said Kori. "And the really cool thing is that we all get to have this unique and intimate experience of seeing someone's home and be invited into their personal space. We wouldn't get that opportunity if we were in the office."

As an icebreaker, the training team helped each LASR prepare a personal tagline that included their name, university, and a list of fun facts about themselves. They shared them with each other as well as with the leaders they met, who in turn offered their own fun facts. It helped the cohort get to know each other better and helped to build a bond that traditionally has developed organically when the LASRs were able to meet on site and grab lunch or take coffee breaks together.

"These LASRs form strong personal relationships inside and outside of their professional environment. They bond. They become a fraternity in a sense and it becomes this big family. I thought we would lose a piece of that to be very honest but they blew my expectations, just as much as their productivity, out of the water," Kori said with a sense of pride and awe.

In fact, the Gen10 LASRs became pioneers for many firsts within the program, creating their own opportunities to create camaraderie in a virtual realm. They brought ideas forward like "Getting to Know You" sessions, small breakout groups whose participants and topics changed weekly. They started their own virtual book club and held meetings to discuss the content. The LASR training team took note and tweaked their own programming to include more small-group collaboration sessions using breakout rooms and giving LASRs the opportunity for in-depth conversations and more personal, individual time together. As the world began to open up, those who lived close to each other started to socialize outside of working hours to continue to build relationships.

When you ask why this generation of LASRs chose Lenovo, the answer is invariably "its people," so it comes as no surprise that friends of the program were integral to its success in the new modality. Kori explains, "I'm so proud of Lenovo and the leaders who embrace the LASR program every year. It takes literally an army of passionate people to make this program successful. When we realized we were going to have to go virtual, I went back to our business unit leaders, to see if they were still willing to be involved virtually, and all of them without hesitation said, 'Absolutely yes, but we're going to have to be creative on how we get them embraced and included to the teams.'"

The crux of that creativity was clear communication. After the initial two weeks of training, all 25 LASRs were assigned a business rotation designed to give them a broader view of Lenovo overall but within key units that align to sales. LASRs were placed in finance, fulfillment, supply chain, product management, marketing, enablement, sales, and more. The LASR team deeply considered what that rotation would look like in a virtual world: What's the approach, how do you mentor, and what's the frequency of one-on-one meetings to make sure the LASRs feel like they are part of the team? Once they developed a plan, Kori and her team made sure managers were prepared to bring them into the fold. They prepared profiles of each LASR and encouraged their managers to share those profiles in a welcome email along with the key projects they would be working on. Those teams responded with overwhelming virtual enthusiasm directed toward their LASR and in essence "tried to hug them through the screen."

The LASRs were also enveloped into the Lenovo culture through other means. LASR Inc. is an alumni-run group that drives communication across LASR cohorts, building community between past and present. The LASR Pals program pairs a previous generation LASR with a current one to encourage mentorship and provide one more friendly face who can answer those questions that they may not want to ask in a formal setting. More than half of the LASRs also are active participants in Lenovo Employee Resource Groups where they can continue to build their network and plug in.

Despite the initial trepidation, the virtual version of LASR had some advantages and some staying power. For example, Kori plans to incorporate video-enabled small-group sessions no matter what form the program primarily takes: "I will continue to do video. LASR is constantly evolving as we transform with technology so we will continue to optimize and update the program. Also, with all of the good feedback from the LASRs, those small-group breakout sessions will consistently be part of the DNA moving forward."

As for the Gen10 cohort, not only were they trailblazers who showed resilience and flexibility as they joined Lenovo, they also were able to build skills that will help them throughout their career in this ever-evolving world in which we live.

Parker Yount, Gen10, shared, "The biggest lesson learned is the virtual working world moves just as fast as the real business world, so the key then becomes removing as many barriers to your success as possible. Constant communication, culture building activities, continual training and experiential learning, and networking allow you to succeed just as much behind a screen as in person."

Conclusion

Meeting culture is often a reflection of a company's organizational culture, and in the world of remote work, that meeting culture sets the tone. When welcoming new employees to the fold, steeping them into the culture of the organization is a critical step, one that requires additional thought and effort in a world that has gone remote. However, with careful planning, clear communication, and people-driven investment, not only is it possible to steep new employees in the values and processes of their new workplace, but it can also spark creativity, with ideas born from the pandemic improving the process and being embraced for the foreseeable future.

Chapter Takeaways

- Organizations have their own culture, and it explains why we often hear "let me show you how we do things around here."
- Meeting culture is a real thing that impacts how we meet and work in organizations.
- The best way to build a positive meeting culture is to engage in the best practices, encourage others to do likewise, and lead others back to the basics of meeting science.
- Businesses keep adapting and hiring in the suddenly remote world, and the virtual meeting is the conduit for onboarding and socializing new employees.

References

Allen, Joseph A., Nale Lehmann-Willenbrock, and Steven G. Rogelberg. 2018. "Let's get this meeting started: Meeting lateness and actual meeting outcomes." *Journal of Organizational Behavior* 39 (8): 1008–1021.

Grensing-Pophal, Lin. 2020. "Hiring new employees during COVID-19." Talent Acquisition. SHRM. https://www.shrm.org/resourcesandtools/hr-topics/talent-acquisition/pages/bringing-new-employees-board-during-covid19.aspx.

Hansen, Jared, and Joseph A. Allen. 2015. "An organizational meeting orientation: The construct, scales, and research propositions. In J. A. Allen, N. Lehmann-Willenbrock, and S. G. Rogelberg (Eds.), *Cambridge handbooks in psychology. The Cambridge handbook of meeting science*, 203–222. Cambridge University Press.

Indeed. 2020. "16 Steps to effective virtual onboarding (with checklist and sample schedule)." Indeed for Employers. https://www.indeed.com/hire/c/info/16-steps-to-effective-virtual-onboarding-with-checklist-and-sample-schedule?aceid=&gclid=CjwKCAjwq_D7BRADEiwAVMDdHoxVdn_ONCfQ2OYDOTJIUK00slF9lSXsOU1GCEp0FU41jRdPRA51IhoCbIIQAvD_BwE.

Mroz, Joseph E., Joseph A. Allen, Dana C. Verhoeven, and Marissa L Shuffler. 2018. "Do we really need another meeting? The science of workplace meetings." *Current Directions in Psychological Science* 27 (6): 484–491.

Mroz, Joseph E., Nicole Landowski, Joseph Andrew Allen, and Cheryl Fernandez. 2019. "Organizational meeting orientation: Setting the stage for team success or failure over time." *Frontiers in psychology* 10: 812.

Ostroff, Cheri, Angelo J. Kinicki, and Rabiah S. Muhammad. 2012. "Organizational culture and climate." In I. Weiner (Ed.), *Handbook of Psychology, Second Edition*. Wiley.

Reisenwitz, Cathy. 2020. "How to successfully implement a no meeting day at your company." *Clockwise Blog*. https://www.getclockwise.com/blog/how-to-successfully-implement-a-no-meeting-day-at-your-company.

SHRM. 2020. "Understanding and developing organization culture." Toolkits. SHRM. https://www.shrm.org/resourcesandtools/tools-and-samples/toolkits/pages/understandinganddevelopingorganizationalculture.aspx.

Tsao, Tai. 2020. "What your meetings say about your company culture." *Culture Amp Blog*. https://www.cultureamp.com/blog/what-your-meetings-say-about-your-company-culture/.

Chapter 12

Empowering Employees on the Tech Front

The Converged Perspective

A s knowledge workers the world over shifted suddenly to virtual operations, their mantra might have echoed Nike's: "Just do it." Thoughtful planning was a luxury few could afford unless they were willing to let business grind to a halt as they established their footing. Silicon Valley tech companies were among the first to send their employees home, conducting what *The Wall Street Journal* called, "A nearly million-person, real-time experiment into whether it is possible to operate a fully remote workforce in the age of the coronavirus" (Copeland and Mickle 2020). You might imagine those in the tech industry would be well-suited to the shift, but that was not necessarily the case. Secrecy around products, high levels of security, and complex in-office equipment setups don't easily transition to a suddenly virtual work environment. When Alphabet Inc., Google's parent company, sent workers home, it was reportedly overrun with employee requests for "work from home" kits – monitors, cables, and other technology (Copeland and Mickle 2020).

Knowledge workers across all industries scrambled, as did their companies, to make remote work . . . well, work. While some employees were able to grab their office necessities before heading home for an indefinite period of time, others simply made do with what they had. The consulting firm Accenture had no more than 10% of their 500,000 employees working remotely prior to the pandemic. By the middle of March, nearly all of them were (Thompson 2020). While they may have had the appropriate equipment, those laptops were sometimes situated on ironing boards as makeshift desks.

This worldwide experiment in virtual work meant that the world became a laboratory for social, behavioral, and organizational scientists like Joe. New questions took on pressing importance such as issues associated with working from home, challenges of suddenly meeting virtually, and the adoption of technology that many were unprepared to adopt. All of these and other areas were suddenly in a natural experiment with years of data *before* the pandemic and new data (and new ways to capture data) flowing in *during* the pandemic. We've already shared some of that throughout this book.

At the time of this writing, we are well into the "work-from-home" world, and businesses are seeking a more thoughtful approach to how they empower their remote employees. Few, if any, could have predicted the complete transformation that occurred, so no one can be blamed for not having a plan for the unthinkable (What, you didn't have an endless stockpile of webcams at the ready?). However, lessons have been learned – sometimes the hard way – on what employees need and what they don't need on the tech front at home.

In this chapter, we will explore:

- The biggest technology barriers for remote workers.
- The importance of having the right tools and why best-in-class organizations are investing in them for their employees.
- What industry experts suggest for navigating the days ahead.

The Tech Tool Challenge for Remote Work

If anything, the pandemic has demonstrated our collective resilience, flexibility, and grit. More than ever, work is not where you go; it's what you do – and we continue to do it from every place imaginable, our living room sofas, our kitchen counters, and even our closets (where we can at least close a door!). All of this is possible thanks to the magic of technology, but that magic can quickly evaporate into thin air if, say, your home Internet can't support the strain of two people working from home and multiple children simultaneously sitting in online classes. You can almost hear the bandwidth creaking. In fact, the demand for faster Internet was so high, most Internet providers could not keep up with people calling in seeking upgrades. This was perhaps most apparent in those automated messages pronouncing "longer than normal wait times due to increased demand."

The tech challenge was and continues to be real for many employees. According to a Demand Metric survey done in the summer of 2020, 95% of those surveyed said they use videoconferencing to communicate for work (Demand Metric 2020). However, nearly 94% of video users (meaning pretty much all of them) are encountering challenges and barriers to using it effectively. In fact, three-quarters of the top eight roadblocks mentioned in the survey are related to technology. Many of these concerns echo Joe's data from Chapter 4 and include:

- Video quality issues
- Technical issues
- Concerns about platform security
- Poor viewer experience

- Having the right equipment
- Difficult-to-use platform

But even the two other barriers mentioned – ones that perhaps might not seem directly related to technology – may be linked to tech as well: video call fatigue and keeping people's attention. The right technology may actually help to solve these two issues as well.

Fighting Fatigue with the Right Equipment

Prior to the pandemic, you may not have given much thought to that little lens embedded in the bezel of your laptop, but when stay-at-home orders went into effect, you may have seen yourself in a new light. That built-in camera that you rarely used was now the conduit to your coworkers, and the image they saw may not have been as sharp as you would have liked. Perhaps your makeshift home office didn't offer a lot of light, so your picture looked really grainy, or the room where you had to work was full of hard surfaces that bounced your voice from wall to wall until it reached a poorly matched built-in microphone that made you sound like you were talking from an echo chamber. The less than stellar audio and picture quality may not have been a big deal if you only used them maybe one day a week, but when that one day became five days, that's when the real problems set in.

"The threshold for viability has gone up," said Scott Wharton, vice president and general manager of the Video Collaboration Group at Logitech, a leader in the videoconferencing industry. Scott points to the role poor-quality equipment can have in the rise of video call fatigue: "In person, your audio and video fidelity are perfectly attuned to how our brains work. Being remote, if you don't get it as close to that as you can, you get really tired."

While some laptops may offer decent video and audio options, not all do, so it's imperative that you assess the quality of both. Imagine if your sound was so muffled that your customer could only make out every other word or if your coworkers can't tell if you're truly angry or simply joking because your video is so fuzzy that they can't make out your facial expressions? The harder it is for your conversation partners to see and hear you, the more taxing the experience becomes for them and the higher the potential for miscommunication. Think about how you want to be received and the impact you want to make.

"There may be an element of wanting to show up in the best possible way for yourself, but also it's a matter of being respectful for someone else," Scott says. In essence, investing in equipment beyond the basics is really more about minding the viewer experience – your higher quality setup actually helps your audience even more than it helps you. They actually get the message you're sending, helping avoid unnecessary questions and moving the meeting forward.

Don't forget that from a scientific perspective, these issues deplete the richness of the medium. As discussed in Chapter 7, media richness theory suggests the better the audio and video, the more likely the message being sent will be received in the way it was intended. So where does it make sense to invest?

Consider an External Webcam

In the first few weeks of the pandemic, webcam sales soared a whopping 179%, according to market researcher NPD Group (Howley 2020). With work from home, distance learning, and telehealth, external webcams became hard to come by, especially those that were rated highly. Some third-party resellers took advantage of the scarcity by jacking up prices to ridiculous heights (Welch 2020). Now that the supply chain has had a chance to catch up with demand, you can now find webcams at a wide range of prices. Not only can you expect an upgrade in image quality, you can also enjoy the increased flexibility of placing it where it suits you best. While many models clip onto the top of monitors or laptop screens, they usually can be mounted on tripods as well, allowing you to place them in spots that make sense for your workflow. If you use multiple monitors, you can set up the camera on a tripod between the two at eye level so you can easily move your gaze from the lens to the screens on either side.

Here are a few things to think about when choosing a webcam:

- **What's the webcam resolution and frame rate?** HD (high definition) video is a must. A resolution of 1080p is a pretty sure bet and one you'll find on most solid webcams. However, if you are looking for an especially crisp image, you may want a 4K webcam. Frame rate determines how smooth or choppy your image is when on a video call. A webcam with 60fps (frames per second) will provide a more natural video feed than a 30fps webcam.

- **Does it have autofocus?** Want to be sure you aren't blurry no matter how close you are to the lens? Look for a webcam that offers autofocus so you'll stay sharp no matter where you move within frame. Less expensive webcams tend to be fixed-focus, which means you have one sweet spot where you appear clearly, but if you move out of it, you'll become fuzzy.

- **Does it adjust to all lighting situations?** Maybe you've found a place for your home office that bathes you in soft, natural light. If so, this feature may not be important to you. However, if you either have an abundance of bright sunlight or suffer from too many shadows, this feature may make or break your shot. An automatic lighting adjustment setting can help you compensate for both harsh as well as dim light – a great solution if your room's natural light varies dramatically depending upon the time of day.

Think About Your Best Audio Options

While we have focused so far on video quality, the way you sound to others is equally if not more important during a video meeting. In fact, many studies indicate that if your audio is just medium to marginal in quality, people are more likely to react negatively as a whole, regardless of how good your video is (Harrell 2020). Further, if you run into bandwidth issues, the first thing people do is turn off the video to see if they can proceed in audio only. We'd probably recommend disconnecting and reconnecting to see if it's a connection issue first because of the *very* meaningful difference between videoconference and teleconference effectiveness. However, if you have bad audio devices, no amount of bandwidth adjusting can make it better.

There is no shortage of external audio options: a standalone microphone that sits on your desk, headphones, headsets, speakerphone pods, and more. The sound quality varies as much as the price, so pay careful attention to reviews. Karin made the mistake of assuming a higher price meant higher quality when she purchased her original lavaliere microphone, one that clips neatly on her lapel. However, after one too many audio drops during calls, she returned the higher-priced version and chose a lower-priced but highly rated model instead. That one is her go-to now, and the sound is clean and crisp.

If you are worried about ambient noise bleeding into your virtual calls, headphones or headsets offer a double advantage. Not only do they keep all of that distracting noise out for your audience, but they also can help you to stay better focused on the meeting and not on the sound of your children arguing over who won that round of Rocket League. Many of the recent models of headphones provide noise-canceling capabilities, so even you won't necessarily hear the background noise. For example, Joe's home office sits at the corner of his home nearest a busy road. With his new headset, the audience and team members can't hear the cars going by, and because of the sound-canceling feature, neither can he.

A quick Web search will turn up an overwhelming list of possibilities, but here are some factors to consider:

- **Will they be comfortable?** If you feel like a headset is squeezing your brain, you likely will not be willing to wear it for long. Think about the style that best suits you: in-ear, on-ear, or over-ear headphones? One or two earpiece headsets? This may require some trial and error to learn what works best for you.

- **How's the audio quality?** HD isn't just for video. It's for audio, too, and it can make a big difference in how you sound.

- **Wired or wireless?** If you don't like to be tethered, wireless headsets may be really appealing. However, the Bluetooth connection can sometimes cause lag. Pay attention to battery life to make sure it'll hold up to a day's worth of calls before it needs a recharge. Wired headsets are usually more affordable and have high sound quality, but they do tie you to your device.

Expand Your Field of View

As we've discussed throughout this book, video makes any virtual meeting better, but we still have fewer visual cues than an in-person experience. However, the size of the screen that we use to participate in those calls can also impact our ability to read body language and navigate through various screens.

An external monitor or two can give you more inputs during a virtual meeting by extending and enlarging the world in which you are operating. It's much easier to read the body language in gallery view when the sizes of the boxes are larger. Plus, you can more easily navigate between windows and applications when there's a more expansive landscape on which to layer them.

A larger external monitor can also ward off some of the physiological ill effects of work from home. In July 2020, Lenovo released results of its global study, "Technology and the Evolving World of Work," which surveyed more than 20,000 remote workers worldwide on their experiences with technology in the workplace and the impact of COVID-19 on their preferences, connectivity, and work/life balance (Lenovo 2020). Seventy-one percent of workers surveyed complained of new or worsening aches and pains like headaches and backaches. Using an external monitor placed at eye level can help relieve some of that strain.

Who Is Paying for It?

The answer to that question has changed as the realities of working from home for a longer-term basis have set in. Prior to COVID-19, Scott Wharton of Logitech saw almost no companies paying for work-from-home equipment for employees on a widespread basis, but now he's seeing maybe half doing so to empower all employees to be able to work well remotely. "Now, not only may you have an obligation to do it but it's also in your best interest to level everyone up. So, I see a lot of companies doing the due diligence and seeing what would work best and either paying for it or shipping it out and supporting it. That's a really big change versus where we were pre–COVID-19."

The results of Lenovo's study of remote workers support that view. Seven in ten employees surveyed globally said they purchased new technology to navigate working remotely. Nearly 40% said they have had to partially or fully fund their own tech upgrades. For those living in the United States, that has translated into an average of $348 to upgrade and improve their technology while working at home due to COVID-19, which is roughly $70 more than the global average.

Although we would both advocate that organizations upgrade their employees' work environment with the technology they need, it cannot be overstated that upgrading is a good idea. Those who upgrade both their tools *and* their behaviors will be standouts in the new suddenly virtual world that we are living in. With this in mind, individuals and organizations should be actively seeking to ensure they are optimizing their virtual communication environment.

Keeping Up with Technology . . . or Not

With the rapidly evolving tech landscape, many workers are raising alarms about their employers' abilities to keep up. In that same Lenovo study of more than 20,000 employed adults, 46% felt that their employers are only middle of the pack or falling behind with their tech needs, while 82% indicated that their employers encounter barriers as they endeavor to keep up to date with new and emerging tech (Lenovo 2020).

Meanwhile, the employees themselves are having a hard time with the steep learning curve as they figure out how to use what they already have. Seventy-nine percent of those surveyed acknowledge having to serve as their own IT person while working from home, and a majority are calling for more tech training to make work-from-home work better (Lenovo 2020). Nearly half expressed an interest in continuing to work remotely, but 65% believe they would do their jobs better if they had better tech skills.

A Story from Karin's Perspective

The tech skills gap came to light during the course of Karin's work with one company that had hired her firm to do virtual sales call training. The company had actually made the effort to ship high-quality webcams to the entire sales force to standardize the image quality when they engaged in virtual meetings. While some employees immediately unpackaged them, plugged them in, and played around with the settings until they found success, a good number of people did not even take them out of the boxes. Why? They were unaware of how to even connect them to their devices, let alone to the videoconferencing platforms they would be used on. Instead, they opted to just continue with what they already knew worked, the audio and video options that were lodged within their laptops. The company's efforts to standardize the way reps visually "showed up" on virtual sales calls were falling short.

Recognizing this, Karin added another component to her coaching. For those folks who were leery of giving the new webcams a try, she spent time talking them through the setup process and watched them come online in real time. The difference between the old image and the vivid new one was dramatic, and once that initial barrier to usage was removed, the reps who originally were reticent promised to never go back. However, this realization would likely never have happened if Karin hadn't provided a small amount of tech training to bring those webcams to life.

Putting the tech in the hands of employees is a big step in the right direction, but don't assume everyone will be willing to figure it out on their own. You may find your well-intentioned investment picks up dust on the shelf if you don't provide enough training to ensure everyone knows how to leverage it.

Upgrading Your Software Skills

To this point, the focus of the chapter has been on the hardware needs that should be addressed to ensure optimal communication in virtual environments. At the same time, the software interface should not be ignored. There's a reason for all those stats we shared in Chapter 1 about the growth of virtual meeting software matter. Because, not all virtual meeting software is created equal and not everyone knows how to use it.

For example, Joe was recently asked to lead a discussion for a group of 40 individuals. It was a collaborative decision-making process, and everyone needed to voice their ideas and jointly come to a final list of input. Using Zoom as the platform, Joe used the breakout room function to divide the large group into small groups, assigning them to what could best be described as virtual huddle rooms where they could chat about key questions and ideas. After a short period of time, Joe closed the breakout rooms and allowed everyone to return to the main session where the key ideas from the breakout groups were shared. To those who are very familiar with this functionality, this may seem run of the mill – nothing all that fancy, but the response from participants in this particular meeting was overwhelmingly positive and a bit surprising. Joe received multiple emails, texts, and phone calls from group participants saying they never knew that could be done and how great Joe did at helping them each feel a part of the process.

The point is that many people are simply unaware of the functions of the current software available to them, and practically every day, there's something new that comes online to take collaboration efforts further. For example, companies like Klaxoon are breaking new ground in the area of virtual collaboration. In talking about Board, Klaxoon's collaborative software product, their CEO Matthieu Beucher described it as: "A new standard in visual collaboration for teamwork. Ten percent of the screen is videoconferencing, while 90% is a co-creation space for projects. In that space, links, photos, sticky notes, and so on can be used to collaborate on the project, problem, or topic at hand. It literally brings everyone onto the same page, rather than a share-the-screen experience."

The important point here is that whether you are using Board, Zoom, Microsoft Teams, Google Groups, Webex, BlueJeans, or any number of other video conference platforms, they all are software with tools that may or may not be useful. Matthieu continued,

"The major pitfall for organizations right now is *not* realizing the opportunity that we have right now to question how we work and just keep doing what we've always done. There are new technologies, new software options, and new skills that need to be developed. The moment is now."

Our advice is not so much about using any specific software that we've mentioned, but rather to get to know the software you are required to use as part of your organization. Figure out all the bells and whistles. Experiment with new ways of meeting by playing around with the software in a low-stakes video call with a few of your teammates. You might discover the next best way to collaborate. Or you might find out that the software that you're using really is antiquated and it's time to try something else.

Best Practices from the Experts

So, what can you do from a tech perspective to make remote meetings work? As companies seek answers for their current state as well as the future, we asked some industry experts to share the best practices they would advocate to provide a solid tech foundation.

Checklists from Our Tech Experts

Company and Checklist Item	Yes or No
Klaxoon	
1. Scale new ways of working by using ready-to-use templates.	[ ] Yes [ ] No
2. Make team synchronization a key part of teamwork to create alignment.	[ ] Yes [ ] No
3. Make virtual meetings/team synchronization more frequent but shorter to allow more space for asynchronous work.	[ ] Yes [ ] No

Company and Checklist Item	Yes or No
4. Include visual management when collaborating as a team remotely.	[ ] Yes [ ] No
5. Make team participation more inclusive by using tools that allow for anonymous idea sharing.	[ ] Yes [ ] No

Lenovo

6. Train your employees not on tech as a tool, but how tech folds into their tasks.	[ ] Yes [ ] No
7. Consider the learning curve employees will face with tech and focus on providing the right tools.	[ ] Yes [ ] No
8. Ensure tech is not a "one-size-fits-all" for work devices.	[ ] Yes [ ] No
9. Invest in products with increased usability through predictive AI/Machine Learning.	[ ] Yes [ ] No
10. Provide software and security updates without getting in the way of employees and underlying their benefits.	[ ] Yes [ ] No

Logitech

11. Think about future-proofing. Avoid a single vendor solution so you can be agile.	[ ] Yes [ ] No
12. Equip your employees with high-quality webcams to reduce mental fatigue.	[ ] Yes [ ] No
13. Choose an audio solution that has built-in echo suppression like a good business-grade headset. Laptop audio typically lets all noises through which can be very distracting to your remote meeting participants.	[ ] Yes [ ] No
14. Have an enterprise-grade video system in the office that can capture all of the people in a conference room with good quality audio and video. Don't just use a webcam (designed for individuals) or have everyone awkwardly huddle around a laptop.	[ ] Yes [ ] No
15. Provide bigger screens like an external monitor to increase inputs.	[ ] Yes [ ] No
TOTAL YES	[ ]

Conclusion

With this checklist in hand, you are prepared to think about and consider whether you and/or your organization have the tech tools needed to succeed in the suddenly virtual world. We recognize that this is an investment in the short term but perhaps an essential one for the future. COVID-19 may have sparked the move to remote, but as organizational leaders assess the next phase, a universal return to everyone working in a colocated office with all of their team seems unlikely. Assuming that virtual and remote work is here to stay in one form or another, investing in that reality may be the difference between success and failure in the suddenly virtual world as well as the "choosing to stay virtual" world that may follow.

Chapter Takeaways

- While an overwhelming majority of knowledge workers are using virtual video for work, a nearly equal percentage report tech challenges that create barriers to using it well.

- Having the right equipment can help fight video fatigue.

- High-quality webcams and headsets can greatly enhance the experience for you and your fellow meeting attendees.

- External monitors can enlarge your field of view and provide more inputs that might be limited by the remote meeting experience.

- Many employees made a personal investment in upgrading their work-from-home equipment without reimbursement from their employers.

- Employees are calling for more tech training to enable them to continue to work efficiently and productively remotely.

References

Copeland, Rob, and Tripp Mickle. 2020. "Silicon Valley was the first to send workers home. It's been messy." *The Wall Street Journal*. https://www.wsj.com/articles/silicon-valley-was-first-to-send-workers-home-its-been-messy-11584190800.

Demand Metric. 2020. "The state of video in remote work survey 2020." Demand Metric. https://www.demandmetric.com/content/state-video-remote-work-2020.

Harrell, Scott L. 2020. "Why audio is more important than video image quality." *VTREP*. https://vtrep.com/audio-is-more-important-than-video-picture-quality/.

Howley, Daniel. 2020. "Americans buying 'historic' amount of computers during coronavirus lockdown." Yahoo!Finance. https://finance.yahoo.com/news/americans-buying-historic-amount-computers-webcams-121043910.html.

Lenovo. 2020. "New Lenovo research: people are working more by not going to work, but worry about home tech, data security, and personal costs." Lenovo StoryHub. https://news.lenovo.com/pressroom/press-releases/new-lenovo-research-people-are-working-more-by-not-going-to-work-but-worry-about-home-tech-data-security-and-personal-costs/.

Thompson, Clive. 2020. "What if working from home goes on...forever?" *The New York Times*. https://www.nytimes.com/interactive/2020/06/09/magazine/remote-work-covid.html.

Welch, Chris. 2020. "Webcams have become impossible to find, and prices are skyrocketing." *The Verge*. https://www.theverge.com/2020/4/9/21199521/webcam-shortage-price-raise-logitech-razer-amazon-best-buy-ebay.

Chapter 13

Managing Virtual Meetings Across Global Cultures

The Converged Perspective

T he potential client was clearly not interested . . . or so it appeared to the head of business development, who was delivering a carefully crafted pitch to his audience on the other side of the world.

After a brief introduction and a smooth transition to sharing his screen, he deftly walked his way through a series of slides designed to excite his prospects with all of the possibilities a partnership would bring. However, any time he paused to see if there were any questions, he only heard crickets. Even when he waited for what felt like an insanely long period of time for a response, everyone remained silent. To make it even more awkward, he was the only one on camera. The people he was presenting to all kept their video off. Was his message resonating? Was anyone even listening?

As we have discussed, virtual communication presents a combination of advantages and challenges, but when those meetings involve people from different cultures, there are a whole host of additional barriers to meeting effectiveness, often linked to a lack of understanding of cultural communication and meeting norms.

For years, virtual communication has been used for communicating across distances and in many cases between individuals in different countries, often with different cultural backgrounds and expectations. As the globalization of economies continues with the information age, the reliance on virtual communication across cultures has increased (Kant 2020). Many people carry around a device in their pocket or purse that can make a phone or video call, which allows for immediate communication pathways to friends, family, colleagues, employees, and employers, no matter where they reside.

At a recent virtual conference, Joe observed that more than 30 countries were represented among the attendees of a given session. Although country and culture *are not* equivalent, this still meant that there were likely a large number of folks whose cultural background served as the lens by which they understood the session. More than one "lost in translation" situation occurred where either the accent was so thick that mutual understanding was difficult, or individuals used different words for the same idea or object (witness the US–UK confusion over what "pants" means). But while the virtual nature of the conference created an additional layer of challenges, there were also myriad opportunities, not the least of which was the richness of an event with dozens of countries represented.

Therefore, in this chapter, we explore:

- What differences exist in how people engage in meetings across the world.
- How these pre–COVID-19 differences look in the suddenly virtual world.
- How to manage cross-cultural virtual meetings.
- Ideas for monitoring our own cultural blind spots.

People Engage in Meetings Differently Across the World

Meeting science started looking at meetings across cultures only in the last decade. In part, this is due to an early German–US partnership. Joe and one of his favorite collaborative colleagues, Professor Dr. Nale Lehmann-Willenbrock, began collaborating in 2012. Nale had a keen interest in studying the interactions of people in meetings. She spent many hours watching and coding every utterance in meetings. Not only that, but Nale is bilingual with near-native English and German capabilities. All this meant that an investigation of German and US meetings was a natural first step for collaboration (Lehmann-Willenbrock, Allen, and Meinecke 2014).

The first study compared meetings that were wholly German or American. The participants in the meetings were not from different countries but were culturally homogeneous. The goal was just to see how groups from different cultures differed in how they met. The kinds of behaviors that emerged were fascinating. Based on more than 5000 behaviors in meetings, German teams appeared to focus more on problem analysis, whereas the US teams focused on solution production. In other words, the German teams want to understand the problem *before* they derive a solution, while their US counterparts were eager to just pick a solution that would probably work and move on. Obviously, there are benefits and problems with either approach to problem-solving.

Additionally, US teams engaged in more positive socioemotional behavior than German teams. US teams would engage in agreement behavior, moving to consensus and support more readily than the German teams. Relatedly, German teams engaged in more counteractive behavior, such as complaining, compared to US teams. Needless to say, Joe used that fact to point out when Nale is clearly being unreasonable because her German culture is showing. But more seriously, knowing these differences means choosing to interact in different ways with US teams versus German teams. More patience with the German teams as problems are discussed while making the US teams slow down and consider the benefits/drawbacks of a rushed solution would be good as well.

Shortly after this first study, some other colleagues started working on meetings across the world (van Eerde and Buengeler 2015). Their study included more than 45 nations and general perspectives across these various locations and cultures, comparing the structural and psychological aspects of meetings across these cultures. Although they did not constrain them to singular culture meetings (i.e. only people from one culture in a meeting being rated), they did receive responses from people across all these cultures, thereby providing the most comprehensive comparison to date. And their findings are fascinating!

Meetings in High-Context versus Low-Context Cultures

Before we reveal those findings, though, it's worth explaining the difference between what are called high-context cultures and low-context cultures. High-context and low-context cultures interpret information in different ways, which can result in misunderstanding when both cultures participate in a meeting together. In low-context cultures (the United States, Germany, and the Netherlands, to name a few), there is an assumption that there is a low level of shared information among meeting participants. Messages are understood to be taken at face value and often communicated explicitly in simple, clear terms. Now in high-context cultures (like Japan, Indonesia, and China, among others), the assumption is that there are many shared reference points. Messages are more nuanced, often implied but not stated. In other words, you are supposed to be able to "read the air" to decode the message.

What happens when these two cultures collide in a meeting? Rather than participants coming away with one version of what happened during the meeting and next steps, there could be multiple versions with people from both cultures assuming that their versions are accurate.

Back to Those findings...

In terms of structural characteristics (e.g. length, size, agenda usage, etc.), most characteristics were similar across cultures—with two notable exceptions. The length of meetings was longer in low-context countries (e.g. United States and other Western countries) and action items were used more in low-context countries. Psychological characteristics of meetings (e.g. perceived satisfaction, effectiveness, turn-taking, feelings of trust, etc.), including perceptions of participation and satisfaction, did not differ across cultures. However, mood perceptions did differ. For example, participants from high-context cultures indicated they felt more anxious compared to low-context cultures. Specifically, respondents in meetings in the Latin European and Middle Eastern (high-context cultures) clusters felt more anxious than those in the Anglo and Germanic (low-context cultures) countries.

These Were All Pre–COVID-19 Differences . . . How Do They Look Now?

Good question! The truth is that culture is *very* resilient. Thus, the cultures are still present, and the trends in terms of actual behavior are likely the same now as they were before the global pandemic. However, more importantly, the pandemic made many folks all over the world into suddenly remote workers who required virtual meetings. The answer is more complicated as we consider the suddenly virtual context.

Virtual meetings across cultures likely exhibit many of the same behaviors just mentioned, but now we add technology and distance to *all* meetings. Further, we must consider the fact that many meetings are multicultural. Thus, unlike the clean monocultural analyses from meeting science, it is a bit messier in real life. More likely, a company that operates in multiple countries will have representatives within those and other countries and cultures. Thus, the overly positive Americans will interact with the somewhat more realistic Germans. Their interactions will require additional understanding, *and* that's true regardless of the virtual environment.

Michael Shehane has been helping businesses bridge the intercultural gaps for years as a communications coach with Lighthouse Communications. He suggests his clients approach virtual intercultural communication as an opportunity to learn: "In a virtual meeting, global team members are figuring out in real-time how to negotiate between the culture of the company's headquarters and the culture where the company's satellite office is. This often frustrates people, because they want to get business done, but it is draining to constantly check their assumptions about how to move through the virtual meeting."

Michael suggests adopting a curious, critical-thinking mindset: "Most people avoid learning about other cultures or assume that their home culture's ways of thinking and behaving are superior because they don't want to question the years of cultural programming that have been unconsciously written into their lives." He recommends that, if you are uncomfortable with another participant's position in a virtual meeting, you should tactfully address the discomfort by questioning out loud, "*Hmm* ... this is going against what I have learned in the past. I'm curious why you think this is a good/bad idea?"

Clock versus Relationship Time

Another difference that matters in the virtual context is the sensitivity to clock versus relationship time. This is true particularly in high-context cultures where there is a greater concern for relationships, and meetings are often gatherings where it matters more that folks are present than whether they arrived on time. But wait a minute. What about a virtual meeting? Does it easily accommodate a fluid start time? Only kind of. The organizer must set a start time for the virtual space, likely be present to start the gathering process, and may even be responsible for starting the meeting. While we recommend opening a call early to create an opportunity for informal, non-business talk before the official start time, the loose relationship certain cultures may have with the clock may not always be taken into account. However, given the research on how people across cultures feel about meeting lateness (van Eerde and Azar 2020), it may be that sensitivity to clock time is more universal than not. Regardless, this issue is not fully accommodated by our virtual tools at this point and probably has created some subtle conflict across cultures.

High versus Low Context in a Virtual Meeting

As we explained, people from low-context cultures communicate messages in a way that is very different from the way people from high-context cultures deliver them, and the assumptions that underlie their approaches can be especially problematic in a virtual world.

If high-context cultures expect participants to "read the air," how do you do that when the air is not shared? Virtual meeting attendees are already at a disadvantage because they have fewer data points to decode the message. A low-context listener may not understand if a message is being delivered by a high-context person. That's why defaulting to a low-context form of communication may be necessary to ensure common understanding.

Bridget Fletcher is the director of communication and intercultural programs at Duke University's Pratt School of Engineering, where she works with graduate students who are largely international. With much of Pratt's instruction moving online as a result of the pandemic, Bridget has been counseling faculty on how to navigate intercultural communication in a virtual setting. One of the best practices she strongly endorses? Clear messaging both before and after the meeting.

Bridget says, "When possible, send material ahead of time so participants can think about what questions they might have before going into the meeting. During a meeting, check for understanding. For faculty, we suggest they ask students to reflect back to them what they feel was just relayed. I also highly recommend sending a follow-up email that summarizes the main points and information discussed."

It's also important to explicitly state the purpose of the meeting so everyone is aware of the goal and can properly assess what their roles should be. Michael Shehane of Lighthouse Communications recommends putting the meeting goal directly into the calendar invite: "If the invitation is not clear regarding your meeting's purpose, global teammates might be confused. They might wonder, 'Do I come prepared to speak or just listen? Do I need to mentally prepare for this discussion? Do I need to be on camera?'" If they arrive unprepared to meet the meeting's objective, it will be difficult to accomplish your goals.

This also points to a particular cultural conundrum – the role of chitchat during a meeting. For participants from cultures that tend to minimize small talk and immediately get down to business, the informal conversation can be confusing. They might be wondering if this a meeting for everyone to get to know each other or is this just a preamble to the heart of the meeting itself? Providing a clear goal and a desired outcome at the beginning is critical to remove any doubts about the meeting's purpose.

Pulling Out Participation in a Global Virtual Meeting

Not only can the geographic distances be vast during a virtual meeting, but the differences in the way attendees prefer to participate in the meeting can be just as wide. For non-native speakers, the idea of asking a question or making a comment verbally can feel intimidating, but often, that is the way meeting leaders in the United States measure engagement.

Bridget Fletcher of Duke recognizes this disconnect. "In person, the way we participate and the expectations around the way we participate look very different depending upon where we are from. When you are working in an online environment, I think those differences become exacerbated. We have to find ways to change the way participation looks to us. I think the Western lens tends to view participation as someone raising their hand and speaking up, but that's not necessarily the case."

Text versions of participation, like polling and chat, can be especially valuable because often non-native speakers feel more confident expressing themselves in written form rather than verbally. However, simply encouraging the use of chat may not be enough to get participants to actually use it. That's why Bridget has a technique to drive its adoption. "For almost every meeting, I will have some kind of warm-up where I ask participants to respond to a very low-stakes question in the chat. Once they do so, they realize, 'Oh, that wasn't so bad. I can do that.'" One of her favorite prompts is the 2020-appropriate "What's your quarantine name?" Turns out, your quarantine name is a combination of your current mood and the last thing you ate. For one of her recent meetings, "Happy Avocado" and "Sleepy Toast" were in attendance.

Participation can also take the form of providing input after the virtual meeting is over. Bridget adds, "Following up with an email and having someone respond to that email with something really meaningful, I think is just as great as having someone say that in a meeting. It just requires us to understand that this is just a more comfortable way for them to participate."

Get Comfortable with That Silence

As alluded to earlier, cultural comfort levels with silence vary widely, and when we are from a culture on the low end of the threshold, we may monopolize airtime and miss opportunities to allow for even participation.

Take a nod from what Bridget does in her virtual classroom with students overseas, "Normally in an in-person classroom, the usual time you are supposed to wait after you ask a question is seven seconds. In a Zoom classroom, I double it." Now, that 14 seconds may feel like an eternity to you, especially if you are from a Western culture where it almost pains you to not fill the void. However, consider all of the factors that make that extra time necessary. First of all, speaking up in a virtual meeting can be daunting, especially if you are a non-native speaker who lacks confidence in your verbal skills in the first place. It may take some time to muster up the courage. Second, think of all the technological hoops that you have to go through—the whole process of unmuting yourself, as well as making the moderator aware that you have something to say. Third, there may be lag as the signal straddles the World Wide Web. Bridget actually counts in her head to almost force herself to wait. Often, though, someone will chime in on the 13th or 14th second.

How to Manage Cross-Cultural Virtual Meetings?

The good news is that managing meetings across cultures in the virtual context is not terribly different from managing singular culture meetings in the same virtual environment. Our first advice is therefore to consult the best practices already outlined. They are generally universal, so the earlier chapters about old and new best practices, as well as on-camera communication tools are a good place to start. However, that's not a fully satisfying answer given the differences just highlighted. Therefore, we do have a few additional things that should be considered when meeting with people from different cultures.

Blind Spots in Virtual Intercultural Communication

One of the first steps you should take is to identify your own cultural blind spots. People have their own set of biases that stem from their upbringing, their personality, and their culture. Therefore, the first recommendation is to be aware of who you are, consider the differences between you and those you are planning to meet with, and seek ways to accommodate those differences subtly and kindly. Most people prefer to not be singled out in terms of their culture or other personal characteristics, particularly in front of colleagues, so being subtle is more about sensitivity, inclusion, and concern for others.

While it is valuable to be introspective, it is also valid to realize that we don't know what we don't know. That's why outside experts can help. For managers of global teams, bringing in an intercultural communication expert can both raise awareness of blind spots but also provide tools to manage their way through them.

Here's some advice from Michael Shehane. "Trainings and workshops with an expert at intercultural communication can provide global teams with experiences that show them and help them feel what productive intercultural communication can be like. These trainings and workshops are also a safe place to ask etiquette and cultural awareness questions. While I believe all parties have best intentions, effective intercultural communication requires modeling, discussion, and practice for people to build habits and put these skills into everyday use."

Managing the Flow

If you are leading the meeting, it is imperative to set some ground rules to help manage the flow of conversation. This is an extension of the best practices related to encouraging open and psychologically safe participation among meeting attendees and leaders. To do so, particularly when multiple cultures and diverse backgrounds are present, set expectations in advance that everyone's input is desired and the degree to which it will be solicited. Will you call on people or simply expect them to participate evenly? That's important to state upfront when dealing with cultures where open participation in meetings may not be as encouraged.

Explicitly stating expectations will also ward off another potential problem. In some cultures, speaking over each other is the norm, but as you are probably well aware, that conversation style does not work in a virtual meeting and leads to clipped audio snippets that contribute nothing. At the outset of the meeting, make clear that people need to wait their turn and not interrupt. However, also be clear how they can get in the conversation queue. Suggest that they raise their virtual emoji hand or their physical hand if the meeting is small enough that you can see everyone on gallery view. You can also ask them to register their interest in talking on chat. That way you can call upon them in an organized fashion and allow everyone's voices to be heard in full.

While we frown upon interruptions, there is one exception that a meeting leader can and should exercise if necessary. If someone is monopolizing and taking the conversation down a nonproductive path, finesse a way to cut in and then give the floor to someone else who has been quiet. This is consistent with our conversation on best practices related to participation, procedural communication, and keeping things on track. However, this becomes more important in virtual meetings where those who are less intimidated by the medium may take up more airtime than others who are less inclined to speak up. As a leader, it's your job to take control of the conversation and drive the meeting forward, and interrupting an errant participant may be the only way to redirect to the purpose at hand.

The Importance of Camera Use in Virtual Intercultural Communication

If a language barrier might exist in a face-to-face meeting with the parties involved, imagine how much more difficult it would be to overcome this when the visual cues are removed. That is just one reason why turning the webcam on is often an essential element of effective virtual meetings across cultures. Video allows you to read lips, facial expressions, and body language. While it's not as easy to do virtually as it is in person, at least it provides some additional inputs that would be absent with audio alone.

Having the camera on also allows you to implement clear signals of assent or disagreement that are universal across cultures. If you are trying to assess how your global attendees feel about a plan of action, you can ask people to raise their hands if they agree. If you are looking for a more nuanced answer, they can use their thumbs as a visual gauge (up = good, sideways = so-so, down = not good), or even use their fingers to provide a rating on a scale from 1 to 5.

However, turning on the camera may not always be possible when meeting virtually with global teammates or partners. Dramatic differences in time zones can be an extra burden for those who drew the short straw on when the meeting was scheduled. While it might be midday for you, it may be the middle of the night for your conversation partner. Would you want to turn your video on during the wee hours of the morning? Inconsistent connectivity can also prove challenging. Perhaps they have enough bandwidth to support an audio feed but adding video results in diminished quality of the call. Opting for audio-only may make the most sense if using the camera threatens their ability to engage in the meeting at all.

Beware of On-Camera Bias

Remember Joe's observations about a virtual meeting where half of the participants were on camera and half had their video off? Joe was stunned to realize that those who had not elected to turn their video on were practically forgotten by those who had decided to have their faces shown. It was not intentional, and once the inadvertent exclusion was recognized, meeting attendees were apologetic. This story highlights a bias that virtual meeting leaders may exhibit; that is, a tendency to pay more attention to those who have their video on.

Turning on the camera may not always be possible, so it is important to ensure that those without video are not ignored. By the same token, those who have turned their webcam on should not be expected to be "uber participants" and shoulder more than their share of the meeting burden. As a leader, cold calling can be an effective tool for creating even participation, but just make sure it is equal opportunity regardless of whether the camera is on or off.

Conclusion

While the world of work became *suddenly* remote, much of that work may become *permanently* remote the world over. Understanding the issues of meetings across cultures will only continue to be important as organizations grow, expand, and progress into the future. This has implications for both the virtual meeting context across cultures as well as the hybridization of meetings. It's easy to imagine a meeting where two people from one culture are colocated and on video speaking with two others in another country who are also colocated on video. Sensitivity to cultural differences will be essential to ensure effective communication and collaboration. Many of the best practices and advice shared in this book are going to be put to the test as new forms of meeting arise, and with that, we turn to our final section of the book where we look at what happens to meetings in the next normal.

Chapter Takeaways

- Meeting characteristics, both structural and psychological, differ based upon the cultural norms of participants.

- When meeting participants come from low-context and high-context cultures, they may come away from the meeting with different versions of events and next steps.

- To overcome intercultural blind spots, adopt a curious, critical-thinking mindset that allows you to check your assumptions.

- For virtual global meetings, explicitly state the purpose of the meeting and its intended goal to eliminate misunderstanding of the desired outcomes.

- Reframe what participation looks like to include ways that are not only verbal.

- Allow for longer periods of silence to encourage participation from global participants.

- Consider bringing in an expert to help leaders of global teams better manage the potential cultural gaps.

- Set ground rules for meeting conversation to avoid interruptions or monopolizing of the dialogue.

- Encourage webcam usage but be cognizant of potential barriers to turning the video on.

- Seek even participation regardless of the camera being on or off.

References

Kant, Vanshica. 2020. "When did globalization begin? The answer might surprise you." World Economic Forum. https://www.weforum.org/agenda/2019/01/when-did-globalization-begin-the-answer-might-surprise-you/.

Lehmann-Willenbrock, Nale, Joseph A. Allen, and Annika L. Meinecke. 2014. "Observing culture: Differences in US-American and German team meeting behaviors." *Group Processes & Intergroup Relations* 17 (2): 252–271.

van Eerde, Wendelien, and Sana Azar. 2020. "Too late? What do you mean? Cultural norms regarding lateness for meetings and appointments." *Cross-Cultural Research* 54 (2–3): 111-129.

van Eerde, Wendelien, and Claudia Buengeler. 2015. "Meetings all over the world: Structural and psychological characteristics of meetings in different countries." In J. A. Allen, N. Lehmann-Willenbrock, & S. G. Rogelberg (Eds.), *The Cambridge Handbook of Meeting Science*, 177–202. Cambridge University Press.

PART FIVE

What's Next in the Suddenly Virtual Meeting World?

D uring the pandemic, there was talk of the next normal, the new normal, getting back to normal, and what will be the normal of the future. Some of the optimistic news agencies started talking about a new normal as early as April 2020 (Aubrey 2020). Our approach mainly takes the perspective of the next normal, seemingly a constantly moving target, making the basis of this book about coping with being suddenly virtual, which was the next normal for many folks and continues to be the status of so many people.

Thus, we return to the purpose for which we started out on the journey in this book. This book provides a science-based guide to optimize the virtual meeting (Chapter 2), talking about the old best practices (Chapter 3), new best practices (Chapter 4), and the on-camera best practices that are both skillable and scalable (Chapters 5 and 6). Throughout these early chapters, the aim is to encourage readers to reflect and consider their own situation and sphere of influence, relative to their virtual meetings and remote work and workers.

We then target a host of opportunities, challenges, and pitfalls of this next normal modality for meetings (Chapters 7 through 13). In these chapters, we tackle everything from professional video etiquette, to organizational culture of onboarding, and the global culture clash with meetings consisting of participants around the world. Perhaps not all of these chapters spoke to you personally, but we hope that some of them have identified opportunities for continued improvement and success.

The final section of this book is geared toward the future of meetings. While we have learned from the experiences of 2020, no one truly knows what tomorrow may bring, let alone the next few years. However, we want to provide you some guidance on what will *likely* be happening next (Chapter 14) and how you can best navigate the meetings of the future, no matter what shape they may take (Chapter 15).

Embracing the Hybrid Meeting

The Converged Perspective

A s the pandemic prompted a sudden shift to virtual meetings and remote work, many started to think about the look of the new or next normal. Some thought that gatherings of people would never be the same. Some argued that the shift to remote showed corporations that they may not need to spend all that money on office buildings. Still others like us started to think about the likelihood that humans will always be human, and fighting human nature is generally futile in the long run. In other words, humans are social creatures.

Citing Maslow's "Hierarchy of Needs," it is generally agreed that humans have psychological needs of belongingness and love (Maslow 1943). This means that one of the more basic needs for all humanity is the need to have friends, intimate relationships, and so forth. For that to occur, we must gather. We must connect and we must fulfill that need. Otherwise, additional and other more complex needs will not have the potential to be met.

When we consider this idea in terms of our suddenly remote world, it is unsurprising that organizations started exploring another shift: the shift from fully virtual to hybrid. Recall that in earlier chapters we defined a hybrid meeting as one in which some people are in one room connecting virtually with others in another room or rooms across distance. Obviously, we'd recommend videoconferencing for the connecting, but the point here is that there are people in small groups, or dyads, interacting with other people in groups or dyads, across distance. And these hybrid meetings existed *before* the pandemic.

A Story from Joe's Perspective

Observation #1: A couple years ago, I was in a staff meeting with a number of different colleagues discussing decisions about education and training. We were gathered together around a conference room table with a very nice speakerphone in the center where a few others were dialed in. I was leading the meeting and kicked things off with a discussion of student needs and issues from recent projects. The conversation was robust and consistent as we marched through the previously shared and cleanly articulated agenda. I was personally quite pleased with how the meeting was going, and even acknowledged that I was following all the best practices for meeting science. Decisions were made concerning the future of students on projects, faculty assignments, and so on. As we proceeded to round up the meeting, someone on the speakerphone cleared his throat, and my heart sank. We held the entire meeting, start to finish, without even inviting anyone on the phone to participate or contribute. I apologized profusely, and thankfully the folks on the call were gracious to me, shared some important points, and the meeting adjourned. It was at that moment I realized that the hybrid meeting was a real thing and I had truly failed at it.

Observation #2: A few weeks ago, I was on a virtual meeting with a client discussing issues related to remote work, with key emphasis on the work–family spillover issue (e.g., kids at home and work being at home and so forth). In this meeting, there was a group of people around a table with a camera showing two people in frame and two out of frame (love social distancing), another three people at their offices in other locations, and me in my home office. Thus, we had a hybrid meeting, and I had learned my lesson (see Observation #1). I invited everyone to have their camera on, which they did, and the meeting proceeded following the agenda and hitting on key topics of concern for the client. As the conversation continued, I started to notice a pattern that I later verified with the recording (I often record my meetings these days for recordkeeping). There was pretty equal participation by camera location. Meaning, each camera had roughly equal amounts of talk time. But, there's a problem here. There were four people on one camera, and then four people total on individual cameras. Five cameras on, but eight people represented, and the participation reflected the cameras, not the relative number of participants. The group of folks participated less per person than the individuals on camera.

These observations demonstrate some challenges with the hybrid meeting both before and during the pandemic, and others have likely had similar experiences. As wonderful as the hybrid meeting and hybrid teams may be, they require yet another set of skills to manage them effectively.

In this chapter, we will explore:

- Some observations from during the pandemic relative to hybrid work.
- How to manage a hybrid team.

- Recognizing work–family conflict in the remote and hybrid work environments.
- Best practices for hybrid meetings.

Observations from the Suddenly Remote World

As the pandemic wore on, surveys started to be done by many different organizations, researchers (like Joe), and consulting groups. These surveys painted a rather interesting picture of how people felt about the work environment, or perhaps, how they felt about their kitchen table setup (or their home office for the lucky few).

In a late summer 2020 survey of 1123 remote workers by *The New York Times* and *Morning Consult*, 86% said they were satisfied with the current arrangements, even when that sometimes meant working from their bedrooms or closets. They reported feeling less stressed, more able to take breaks, and that they were spending more time outdoors (Strzemien et al. 2020).

Only 1 in 5 of those workers wanted to go back to the office, and 1 in 3 would even move to a new city or state if remote work continued indefinitely. For those who live in one city, with family some distance away, perhaps a great distance away, remote work forever would allow them to move closer to family. It might reduce or remove commutes entirely for many people. Additionally, those more frequent breaks might result in more walks (40% indicated this) or simply more exercising (33% suggested this), which has implications for insurance premiums and the overall well-being of employees.

However, the pandemic blurred the lines of work and home and changed the way we view our coworkers, perhaps forever. In another survey of 2000 remote workers in 6 countries, over 60% of people said they feel more empathetic toward their colleagues now that they have a better view of life at home (Spataro 2020). Yet, in *The New York Times* survey, 35% of moms and 20% of dads said that remote work made it *more* difficult to balance work and home duties. Thus, we build empathy, while pulling our hair out trying to be all that we must be for children, pets, or other dependents.

Meanwhile, fully remote feels more inclusive for some. Over half (52%) of the people that were surveyed feel more valued or included as a remote contributor in meetings because everyone is now in the same virtual room (Spataro 2020). This was recently confirmed in some of Joe's new data on virtual meetings. Across a pilot sample of 100 virtual meetings, Joe found that participation flow appeared to be more equal in virtual meetings compared to face-to-face meetings from before the pandemic. In other words, the distribution of participation appears to be more equal, and this makes sense because, in the virtual meeting room, there is no head of the table nor even the power positions on the sides of oval tables. That's all gone. Sure, maybe the fanciest background gets a few comments, but that doesn't change the fact that everyone is a talking head and no one truly stands out. However, this inclusivity aspect of virtual meetings needs to be further tested and verified scientifically.

With the good and the bad, some might begin to wonder whether the physical office space will disappear with a suddenly large number of vacant commercial properties. Well, looking in at the managers in that same surveyed sample, 82% of managers expect to have more flexible work-from-home policies post-pandemic. So, even if people and organizations are making the transition back, it is likely some remote work is going to continue. Further, at least for a while (and maybe longer), the days of going to work sick to be a "good soldier and work through it" are *gone*.

Many organizations recognize that a return to the office will most likely not mean a return to business as usual and are taking a proactive approach to learn what their employees hope their work life will look like post-pandemic. At SAS Institute, whose company culture consistently garners them spots on "Great Places to Work" lists the world over, they've been surveying their employees to better understand how they would like to work and how they can best support them by asking them questions like, "When we return to work, what is your ideal situation? Do you want to be in the office full time? Do you want a hybrid? What would make your situation easier?"

According to Shannon Heath, corporate and executive communications specialist at SAS, it comes down to listening to your employees: "I think SAS really understands that and wants to make the best of both worlds because we do have a beautiful campus with a lot of amenities. It was designed for a purpose to be that way. We don't want to lose that because it's a big part of our culture, but that's why I think a hybrid approach will be the best of both worlds. That way those who want to be in the office all the time can be there. Those who want to be there part time can be there and still enjoy the culture that we have built, but then let that culture spill over to our remote work as well."

We tend to agree with a statement from Scott Wharton from Logitech that in the not-too-distant future, "All meetings will be some combination of some people remote and some people in an office somewhere, so I think it's going to be really important to think about how you can support both sides of the equation." In other words, we would sum up the suddenly remote world as following this pattern:

- Pre–COVID-19 Pandemic: Almost everyone is in the office, and you have to "dial some people in." The exceptions are when collaborating with or working with folks across large distances or around the global economy. Many, though not all, of those meetings were virtual.

- During–COVID-19 Pandemic: Everyone is at home participating in meetings virtually.

- Post–COVID-19 Pandemic: Some people are at home, some in the office, some across the country, some around the world, and most meetings have face-to-face and virtual components. The hybrid meeting reigns.

Assuming this pattern emerges for some or many organizations, there are a variety of considerations that we now turn our attention toward.

What Does a Hybrid Meeting Look Like?

Prior to the pandemic, most companies had designated places for meetings on-site: large conference rooms for gatherings of 10 or more and maybe huddle rooms for smaller group work. While some of these rooms were equipped for videoconferencing, the majority were not. When stay-at-home orders went into effect, all of those on-premise conference rooms went dark. In turn, ring lights went on in homes all over the world, illuminating the faces of those suddenly virtual employees who embraced video meetings via webcam.

The hybrid meeting combines both of those scenarios but also likely incorporates a multitude of other physical spaces that are still being explored. Massimo Rapparini is the CIO at Logitech and also oversees the company's real estate in more than 30 countries. With his dual role, he knows firsthand the decisions many of Logitech's customers are trying to make.

"What we realize is there's going to be a whole shift in terms of the types of meeting rooms, the spaces we create for people to meet, where you make meeting technology available physically – in a specific pod or even in a corridor," Massimo says. "And you have to couple that with the equipment that people want and need to have at home in order to have these virtual meetings as well." He sees a growing demand for a wider variety of different settings, a much more diverse set of environments that allow the hybrid meeting to happen.

The complexity of the IT infrastructure to support all of those environments requires an agile ecosystem that enables work from anywhere. Logitech already had a strong baseline of remote work as long-time evangelists of video collaboration for years, but even they faced a learning journey that continues to this day. According to Massimo, "It's definitely opened our eyes to the need for that flexibility that we are trying to build. It's a whole different way of working. It's driven a need to be much more engaged and much more matched with our employees to their way of working . . . understanding that something you assumed will work in all situations now needs to be complemented with other tools."

How to Manage a Hybrid Team

Creating the hybrid meeting environment is one thing, but managing the people within it is an entirely different challenge. While hybrid teams work much like colocated teams, additional effort is needed by the team leader and the team members to ensure that the team functions well. In October 2020, once it became clear that the pandemic was not abating and that new work approaches were here to stay, articles started to pop up in popular management press concerning the "do's" and "don'ts" of managing hybrid teams (Knight 2020).

It may now come as no surprise that these recommendations are highly consistent with the general principles for good management of teams (SHRM 2020) as well as some new nuances that are unique to the suddenly virtual world. For example, one of the do's mentioned is "set clear priorities and objectives so that everyone on your team focuses on what's most important" (Knight 2020). Team leaders, managers, and members would likely all agree that setting goals and priorities, as well as assisting the team in staying on track toward those goals is a best practice for *all* teams in all working contexts, generally.

In contrast, the "do" to "be inclusive" for hybrid teams includes holding all team meetings online so everyone is on equal footing and feels a part of the meeting. As Joe's observation demonstrated, keeping track of those online while engaging with the people in the room is difficult. One strategy and suggested best practice may be to send folks that are colocated back to their respective offices, thereby having *all* attendees in their individual boxes on the virtual meeting screen. Some might consider this an avoidance strategy, but it is an effective one if it becomes apparent that either the in-person or the online folks are dominating the meetings.

In terms of "don'ts," the early guidance includes don't be rigid, don't ignore signs of stress, and don't forget to have fun (Knight 2020). However, it might be easier to understand the opposite to these don'ts, which is *do* be flexible in this ambiguous situation as new work processes are learned. Do be empathetic, particularly as you learn of the challenges and struggles of your teammates. Depending on someone's life situation, hybrid work may be wonderful or miserable. Do have fun by getting to know your team, connecting in these hybrid meetings, and, as we've said before, allow the interruptions or challenges of remote and hybrid work to be something of a shared experience that we can hopefully laugh about as things normalize.

Underlying these do's and don'ts of the hybrid team management approach is an overt concern for employee well-being and the need to mitigate burnout. It is to this issue we turn now as we consider the challenges of work–family spillover.

How to Mitigate Work–Family Spillover

A major concern that arose as people transitioned to remote work and that might continue into hybrid work is work–family spillover.

In our descriptions of "Zooming" from the kitchen table while our kids worked on their remote schoolwork, the possibility of work getting in the way of family needs – and vice versa – was apparent.

Work–family spillover happens when behaviors, stress, moods, and emotions that arise during work are transferred to the family domain (Mennino, Rubin, and Brayfield 2005). These behaviors and affective states (i.e. moods, emotions, and stress) can have wonderful and harmful effects on home life. For example, getting a promotion with an associated raise can be reason for celebration at home, whereas dealing with a disgruntled colleague can create venting behavior and stress-induced coping that may or may not be positive.

Now, let's throw a pandemic into the mix, move most knowledge workers to home offices (or the kitchen table, closet, or couch), and see if we *don't* see work–family spillover. Yeah, right, no problem there. And if that sarcastic statement isn't enough, let's add that the entire family, at least for a good portion of the pandemic, has to also be at home doing their respective work or school. In short, the home became a hotbed for work–family spillover and conflict.

A Story from Joe's Perspective

Since the pandemic began, I was one of the lucky few who had a designated office space at my home that I could go to and work. In most cases, this helped me because I was able to close the door and engage in my workplace meetings. Given the nature of my work, and laws protecting student data and patient data, it was truly important that I had this space to retreat to for many of my daily interactions.

Yet, I cannot begin to count how many times my wonderful, beautiful, seven-year-old daughter felt it necessary to come in and give me a hug. She's a hugger. About half the time, she would also get to wave at whoever was on the video call with me, and it became a running joke with some of my colleagues and students (e.g. "When will we see your little sweetheart today!?").

Reflecting on it now, I'm embarrassed to say that I began to be annoyed with my seven-year-old. She's wonderful, but time and again, she would come in, want a hug, and wave at the people on the screen. It was a game to her, and I had had enough. After lecturing her on the importance of not bothering Daddy while he's working, I had several hours and even days of uninterrupted virtual meeting time.

And at the end of that time, I realized I had allowed the work to spill over and impact my family. I then found myself apologizing to my daughter, thanking her for the hugs, and asking her to listen at the door. If she doesn't hear me talking, she should go ahead and come in and give me those most precious hugs. Now, she doesn't come in as often as before, but the resumption of those hugs was a meaningful reminder that the spillover can take away precious moments and we have to be careful of the conflict and damage they can cause."

Given Joe's perspective, and given the body of scientific evidence on the negative effects of work–family spillover on employee and family well-being (Sirgy et al. 2019), we recommend a few simple strategies here to mitigate the problem.

1. First, respect your own and others' family and "after-hours" time. Yes, in a global economy and workplace, you might have to take the occasional early morning or later evening call. But, for the most part, don't get in the habit of organizing or encouraging others to organize meetings at these times, when avoidable.

2. Second, consider embracing the hybrid work phenomenon. When in the office, have the meetings, the sensitive conversations, and the synchronous work activities. When out of the

office, reduce the meetings, avoid sensitive conversations that could be overheard, and engage in the asynchronous activities that need to be done.

3. Third, remember to be sensitive to the needs of family and home life, and do not short-change it. Most coping efforts, recovery needs, and self-care behaviors occur outside normal business hours during our home time. If we ignore those needs, we might be turning away a warm hug from a seven-year-old who just loves you and wants you to smile.

Hybrid Work and Best Practices for Hybrid Meetings

When asked about the future of work, Matthieu Beucher, CEO of Klaxoon, said, "For hybrid work, with people that are two days in the office and three days at home, for example, most importantly, teams need tools to support that type of synchronous and asynchronous work. That is the next competitive advantage." Not having the right tools and a well-planned approach to empower the hybrid workforce could jeopardize your business, considering that the early evidence suggests hybrid work situations are here and may stay for the foreseeable future. With that in mind, let's spend some time looking at the best practices for hybrid meetings.

Build on Best Practices Already in Place

Hybrid meetings do not require a whole new set of rules. First, all the old meeting science best practices still apply, as do most of the new virtual meeting science findings. Second, pretty much all of the on-camera best practices still apply for hybrid meetings. We still strongly recommend that in all virtual meetings, you *turn the camera on.* Previous chapters do a great job of discussing these practices and we would encourage you to consider them once again here as you think about the hybrid work situations that you may or may not find yourself in.

However, just as the do's and don'ts for hybrid teams included some new and unique nuances for effective team management, best practices for hybrid meetings consider a few additional opportunities and challenges. These stem from Joe's observations that we shared at the beginning of the chapter. There are two major considerations.

Dealing with Subgroups of Participants

As the first observation demonstrated, two groups of folks emerged: one on the phone and one in the room. Those who were joining by phone could not interact effectively with each other or with the other group without strong facilitation, and that's why the burden or opportunity rests with the leader. Probably the first thing to do is to remember the folks on the virtual side of the meeting. Video will help with that, but even then, it is not uncommon for people to see what's in front of them in the form of a person and be distracted away from the people on the screen. Enabling the virtual attendees' participation is a skill that will develop with time. If you're the meeting leader, you can put reminders on the agenda or perhaps even assign a colocated person to assist with asking the virtual participants for input, thoughts, and feedback. Thus, remembering and engaging with online participants can become both a priority of the meeting leader and a role within the meeting for an attendee.

Managing the New Side Conversations

In these new hybrid situations, it is likely that a few folks in one location are communicating with a few others in another location.

This can lead to meeting fracturing, which is the process by which larger groups fracture into smaller discussion groups. Now, meeting fracturing is not necessarily a bad thing. Side conversations – ones that are on-topic – can help get important information into the main dialogue, which in turn allows for better decision-making. However, when those side conversations run off-topic or become excessive, they can harm the effectiveness of the meeting in achieving the defined goals. Thus, both the meeting leader and attendees need to be careful not to engage in side conversations and fracture the meeting along the virtual communication lines; those in the same physical room can begin talking among themselves, leaving those joining virtually out of the conversation. When that happens, rather than a collaborative meeting with all participants, you have several small meetings occurring simultaneously with a camera on.

Overall, the key is to be mindful of the new interpersonal group dynamics that are present in hybrid meetings that are not present in standard virtual meetings, nor in the typical face-to-face meetings. Further, it is possible to embrace these hybrid meetings as an opportunity to get naturally existing subgroups to collaboratively contribute to the overall team performance. Let the side conversations and the meeting fracturing enable performance, so long as any virtue gained does not exceed into a vice of inefficiency.

Conclusion

If trends hold, the hybrid work environment and the hybrid meeting will be core components of how many businesses work. While a hybrid model brings flexibility and agility, it also brings challenges, especially for those who are tasked with leading teams that are composed of colocated and remote workers. When in doubt, look to the old and new best practices based in meeting science. However, be on the lookout for burnout – leaving the office is easier when it isn't housed under your own roof. In the next chapter, we leave you with some final thoughts on the forever altered role of meetings and the work that drives them, but also give you an opportunity to roll up your sleeves and apply all that you've learned over the course of reading this book.

Chapter Takeaways

- For many organizations, hybrid meetings will become the norm with a combination of participants in the office as well as those who are remote.

- Businesses may need to rethink their on-premise meeting spaces and the technology placed in them to enable hybrid meetings.

- Most best practices for all meetings hold true for hybrid meetings – with some nuance. For example, in order to level the playing field, consider having everyone join a hybrid meeting online using their webcams, so everyone appears in their own individual boxes.

- Work–family spillover may continue to be an issue for hybrid teams and needs to be attended to in order to mitigate burnout.

- Meeting leaders should prioritize remembering and engaging online participants rather than focusing solely on those colocated.

- Beware of counterproductive side conversations that can develop along virtual lines during hybrid meetings.

References

Knight, Rebecca. 2020. "How to manage a hybrid team." *Harvard Business Review*. https://hbr.org/2020/10/how-to-manage-a-hybrid-team?utm_medium=email&utm_source=newsletter_daily&utm_campaign=mtod_notactsubs.

Maslow, A.H. 1943. "A theory of human motivation." *Psychological Review* 50 (4): 370–396.

Mennino, Sue Falter, Beth A. Rubin, and April Brayfield. 2005. "Home-to-job and job-to-home spillover: The impact of company policies and workplace culture." *The Sociological Quarterly* 46 (1): 107–135.

SHRM. 2020. "Developing and sustaining high-performance work teams." Toolkits. SHRM. https://www.shrm.org/resourcesandtools/tools-and-samples/toolkits/pages/developingandsustaininghigh-performanceworkteams.aspx.

Sirgy, M. Joseph, Dong-Jin Lee, Seolwoo Park, Mohsen Joshanloo, and Minyoung Kim. 2019. "Work–family spillover and subjective well-being: The moderating role of coping strategies." *Journal of Happiness Studies* 21 (8): 2909–2929.

Spataro, Jared. 2020. "The future of work—the good, the challenging and the unknown." *Microsoft 365 Blog.* https://www.microsoft.com/en-us/microsoft-365/blog/2020/07/08/future-work-good-challenging-unknown/.

Strzemien, Anya, Jessica Bennett, Tracy Ma, and Eve Lyons. 2020. "Out of office: A survey of our new work lives." *The New York Times.* https://www.nytimes.com/2020/08/20/style/working-from-home.html.

Chapter 15

Preparing for the Next Normal in Our Suddenly Virtual Meetings

The Converged Perspective

N ow, here we are, perhaps in the next normal, perhaps expecting another normal down the line. For so many of us (more likely all of us) who were caught unawares by the dramatic impact the pandemic would have on our work lives, the desire to plan for future disruptions is very real. Unfortunately, no one has a way to predict with absolute certainty what we need to plan *for*.

The good news is best practices for making any meeting work are relatively resilient to change. Sure, they may require some adjusting and tweaking to fit a new dynamic, like a more targeted purpose or a different cadence. For example, when an organization moves to mostly remote operations, perhaps the biweekly team meeting needs to be a twice-a-week team meeting to ensure everyone is aware of project progress and priorities. However, the crux of what makes meetings effective in moving business forward is adhering to science-based principles that have stood the test of time. But the gravitational pull to revert to bad habits is strong.

In this, our final chapter, we hope you will turn the magnifying glass on yourself and your team meetings, regardless of the current form they are taking. We begin with a discussion of common pitfalls that will diminish the value of any meeting and how to mitigate the risk of falling prey to them. Then, we ask you to look back on all of the checklists you've filled out over the past chapters and use them to complete a framework to make your meetings better *today*.

Then, we'll close with a bit of prognostication. While we don't purport to have the ability to see into the future, we do call upon the expertise of some industry leaders who shine some light on what role technology will play in meetings on the not-so-distant horizon.

Thus, in this chapter, we explore:

- The fact that we are human and fall into bad habits.

- How we can rid ourselves and others of bad habits.

- Share a framework for reflecting and improving over time.

- The future of our suddenly virtual world.

Caution, You're Only Human

Public service announcement: we are only human. Thus, we are truly creatures of habit (Newby-Clark 2009). This is a wonderful thing and generally adaptive. It means we build routines into our lives. These routines are habits that allow us to function efficiently and effectively. For example, have you ever been so preoccupied with the events of the day that you found yourself sitting at the breakfast table eating your cereal and can't recall all the steps that got you to the table? Or have you ever been on "autopilot" in the car, found yourself halfway to your work office, and then realized you were actually trying to go to the grocery store? In the breakfast situation, your habits and routines allowed you to daydream or think and still get food. In the driving situation, your habit actually delayed you accomplishing what you wanted to accomplish.

Just like our daily morning routines or typical driving patterns, we have habits around how we meet. For example, back in the office, you probably have a conference room for regular meetings. If you walked into that room with Karin, you could probably tell her who sits in what seat for your weekly staff meeting. You could also probably recall a time when someone sat in your seat and it annoyed you. That's because you have habits. Habits are also why, after the first week when Joe learns the names of the students in his class, he knows where to look to find them since they always sit in the same spot. Want to mess with your professor? Never sit in the same place twice. If they take the time to learn names, this will drive them a little nuttier.

And, just like the good and bad habits we have in our daily lives, we have good and bad habits with meetings and virtual meetings. During the latter, people can get into a habit of not turning on their camera or a habit of showing up late to the virtual meeting without a meaningful excuse (Mroz and Allen 2020). Similarly, you can get into the habit of speaking up in your virtual meetings and inviting your quiet colleague to do the same.

Humans create habits *extremely* fast. One lecture, and the students always sit in the same seat. One meeting, and you know who the long-winded person is on your team, as well as the people who will question everything, agree with anything, or zone out during the meeting.

And once habits emerge, they are hard to break. Perhaps you've experienced the bliss and remorse of a New Year's exercise or diet resolution that lasted a day, a week, or even a month (overachiever). The same thing happens with our virtual meetings. You start with a team where two-thirds of them have their cameras off. As the meeting leader, you invite them to turn on their cameras. They do it for the rest of that meeting. Next meeting, 9 times out of 10, they will once again start with their cameras off. Persistence in requesting is one of a few ways to help break the bad habit and build the new on-camera habit.

How to Extinguish Bad Meeting Habits

Psychologists have been studying habits and human behavioral routines for literally hundreds of years. In that research, they found that people easily slip back into bad habits. Sure, much of that research focuses on habits that have physiological and psychological connections (e.g. addiction). But organizational psychologists like Joe have focused on the bad habits at work, including counterproductive meeting behaviors we've already discussed.

The reason we fall back into bad habits is because it's what we are used to, it's our equilibrium, it's our routine, and it's not gone *too* far awry so far. Furthermore, in the midst of having changed the bad habit, humans often find themselves engaging in justification. They may think or even say out loud: "I'll never go back to my old behavior" or "I can bend the rules once and still be okay" or "I'm a different person than I was back then." The reality is that with the right set of cues, the habit will come back and be stronger than ever (or at least as strong as before) (Gillihan 2015).

Falling back into a bad habit with your virtual meetings is consistent with the Psychology 101 topic of operant conditioning. Operant conditioning is the idea that people behave the way they do because of the rewards and punishments present in their environment. They leave the camera off because, by doing so, they get the reward of being able to check out and clean up that inbox (reward). They show up late because it means they don't have to interact with their "work nemesis" (avoid a perceived punishment). The good news is that people can use operant conditioning to eliminate the bad behavior of themselves or others in their virtual (or nonvirtual) meetings. Here are a few examples:

How to Stop the Perpetually Late Person

At some level, the person arriving late feels rewarded or avoids a negative stimulus by arriving late. So, in order to get them to stop, the reward for arriving on time *or* the punishment for arriving late must *exceed* the reward or punishment of the late behavior. This is why some early morning meetings include coffee and donuts. You thought it was for the sweet-toothed boss (and it might be a little bit), but far fewer people arrive late to those meetings than early morning meanings without coffee and donuts.

Obviously, in a virtual world, gathering over a box of donuts isn't possible. However, you can choose to not let that person's lateness interrupt your meeting flow. Do not feel the need to "catch someone up." That would be a reward. The proper punishment is largely dependent upon your particular situation. Recent science on meeting lateness suggests that sanctioning a late person is more common and likely more appropriate when the late person does not provide an appropriate excuse and apology (Mroz and Allen 2020). For example, excuses that are outside the individual's control (e.g. wreck on the freeway) minimize the effect of their lateness. However, excuses within their control (e.g. just got busy doing something on my computer) have a substantial negative impact on the meeting. Thus, depending upon the nature of the lateness, the appropriate "punishment" may simply be starting on time or as complex as official workplace sanction processes (e.g. verbal warning).

How to End Monologues and Keep Participation Equality

Honestly, some people enjoy hearing themselves talk. There's a bit of science to that (i.e. the babble effect). But it can derail a meeting, particularly a virtual meeting where side conversations (except in the chat) are not possible. Well, they are personally rewarded by hearing their voice, so a kind but well-positioned sanction (i.e. punishment) will likely change that behavior. Oftentimes this can be accomplished when the leader draws attention to the verbosity. For example, they might say, for example, "Bob, thank you for your input. I'd like to bring some more folks into the conversation whom we haven't heard from so we can get a full picture of what everyone is thinking. Rick, what are your thoughts?" With repeated implementation of that negative stimulus, over time it will shape the behavior away.

How to Identify Complaining Cycles and Stop Them

For this one, you have to be able to be present while keeping enough cognitive load free to notice the behavior. A complaining cycle begins when someone makes a complaint, someone agrees, then someone adds to the complaint, and then another person agrees, and so on. If you hear a complaint, that's your cue to pay attention to behaviors, both yours and others. Venting is pleasurable. It takes away negative emotions from the complainer and spreads them out over everyone. Others catch that feeling and join in. As soon as you see it, drop a procedural statement, but do so in a way that brings a rewarding tone to it. For example, the complaining cycle is on, and someone jumps in and says, "You know, based on that idea, I think the problem at hand could be solved if we did this [fill in the blank solution]." It gets the complaining to stop and serves to reward individuals away from doing it in the future.

How to Build Rapport and Foster the Humor Habit

Humor has the potential to be a social lubricant to optimize team effectiveness (Yoerger et al. 2017). However, this is the case only if it's affiliative humor, that is, humor that helps to build rapport, that encourages others and does not put down or belittle anyone. The good habit here is positive, affiliative, even inside-joke-type humor and that should be encouraged, rewarded, and maybe even get a laugh (depending upon how corny it is). But, if the humor is put-down humor or targeting those in the room (or even those not in the room), it perpetuates negative socioemotional behavior in the meeting and needs to be extinguished. For this kind of humor, Joe has found that a one-on-one after the meeting with the person lobbing the inappropriate joke is often necessary.

Extinguishing Bad Habits Makes Room for Good Habit Forming

The good news is that the efforts to change our own or others' bad meeting habits opens the door to making good habits. One of the best ways to break a bad habit is to replace it with a good one (Shortsleeve 2018). Sometimes, like with all the bad habit examples we just shared, when the bad habit is gone, the good habit sort of just works its way into rotation.

In other cases, getting rid of the bad habit might leave a vacancy in your behavior during meetings. Perhaps you realize you're the one who likes to monologue during the meeting. Well, if you stop that behavior, what do you do? Or if you help someone else get rid of that behavior, they may feel lost in subsequent meetings. You need to give them something to do. A good habit for them might be to record the minutes or the action items or be responsible for monitoring equality of participation or sharing. We've found that when someone stops a bad habit, giving them something to do instead ensures they are less likely to fall back into that bad habit.

The research is consistent in saying that bad habits come back when stress levels increase (Shortsleeve 2018). Finding ways to reduce stress is important. As we've already addressed the issue of virtual meeting fatigue, we won't revisit that here. Instead, there's another, unexpected side effect of virtual meeting fatigue and the dangerous combination of stressors that arose during the pandemic in 2020. Tammy Chen, DDS, a contributor for Yahoo!, wrote an article concerning a parallel epidemic that occurred in dentistry during the COVID-19 pandemic (Chen 2020). Dentists, like many services, were initially hit pretty hard by the economic shutdown. Only emergency services were provided for a few months. And yet, many dentists were busier than ever responding to emergency needs. Quoting a friend, Tammy wrote, "I've seen more tooth fractures in the last six weeks than in the previous six years" (Chen 2020). The explanation? People were grinding their teeth as a result of stress from all the combined sources of stress in 2020, including virtual meeting fatigue.

Looking in the Mirror: The Adaptive Improvement Model (AIM) Framework

Equipped with the knowledge that human nature will fight our efforts to engage in better behavior, we call your attention back to all those checklists earlier in the book. If you completed them at that time, you've begun the process of "looking in the mirror" and reflecting on your own experiences and opportunities in your virtual meetings. If you have not yet completed them, take a moment, turn back to those chapters, and proceed to reflect on your meeting experiences.

Armed with your reflections, you are now prepared to consider the Adaptive Improvement Model (AIM). The adaptive improvement model is known by many other names in business, including continuous improvement and total quality management. However, AIM is meant to be applicable across all levels, meaning individuals, teams, managers, and organizations could essentially use the same approach in a collaborative way. AIM requires the consideration of three key ideas: things to continue doing, things to stop doing, and things to start doing. For ease of describing AIM, we focus on the individual level, but one could just as easily replace "I" with "we/us" or even "our organization."

1. **Continue.** In the AIM framework, "continue" refers to those things that are happening or being done that one should keep doing. In essence, an individual should ask, "What am I doing in relation to my virtual meetings that I need to continue doing?" Answers could include turning on the camera, making appropriate eye-contact, setting up a professional background, establishing ground rules for the team, and so on. The key idea here is that most individuals, teams, and organizations are doing some good and appropriate things that optimize their suddenly virtual meeting and remote work environment. We mustn't abandon what is working, and perhaps we should even celebrate our efforts a bit. It's too easy to get down on ourselves when it comes to yet another thing to do. Thus, we start with a pat on the back. You're doing great!

2. **Stop.** In AIM, "stop" refers to those things that are being done that should not be done or should be stopped immediately in order to mitigate and remove virtual meeting behaviors, processes, and procedures that are hampering effectiveness and even augmenting virtual meeting fatigue. For example, an individual should ask, "What am I doing in relation to my

virtual meetings that I need to stop doing?" Answers might include stop complaining in meetings, leaving the mute on (or off depending upon the circumstance), multi-tasking, or hindering others' participation. Again, the key idea here is that sometimes we engage in survival tactics when we are dealing with a challenging situation (e.g. back-to-back meetings with no recovery time), and our go-to tactics (e.g. disengaging in the meeting and cleaning the email inbox) are not helpful to the long-term function of the individual, team, or organization.

3. **Start.** "Start" in AIM refers to those things that individuals, teams, managers, and organizations need to start doing to further optimize their virtual meetings and stave off virtual meeting fatigue. For example, an individual should ask "What should I start doing to help improve my virtual meeting experiences?" Answers include many of the things contained in Chapters 3 through 6 and beyond, and are likely unique to each individual, team, manager, and organization. Building upon the reflection checklists you just completed, identify things to start doing, consider the resources needed to make those solutions a reality, and ultimately plan ways to make all your meetings just a bit better.

Given these three sections of AIM, and having hopefully just completed some serious reflection on the provided checklists and your current situation, you are prepared (and perhaps your team with you) to complete the AIM worksheet provided here. Again, the goal is to complete each of the boxes, celebrate the things that you are doing well (continue), identify the things that need to end (stop), and commit to the things that need to begin (start). As you do this, consider the various opportunities and barriers to success. Doing so will ensure that foreseen barriers and opportunities for success are integrated into the plan.

CONTINUE

STOP

START

The Future of Meetings: Looking into the Crystal Ball

As most of us never envisioned a work world that would be suddenly virtual, prognosticating about what's next may seem a bit foolhardy. However, plenty of forward-thinking folks are planning for what meetings may look like beyond tomorrow's next normal.

Given the value that video brings, as established by the reliance upon videoconferencing during the pandemic, let's assume that video communication will maintain its strong foothold. However, technology may shape how video is woven into the way we meet beyond what most of us can imagine today.

Jeremy Bailenson is a professor of communication at Stanford University who studies virtual reality, and he envisions a video-conferencing experience using augmented reality (A/R) glasses to allow us to join meetings with hologram participants. Bailenson told

The New York Times Magazine, "It'll solve a lot of these problems that we're talking about today, because it'll make a meeting feel so much more like a real meeting. It's because it's going to feel like there's somebody in your room" (Thompson 2020). But A/R glasses are just one innovation being considered.

What about those video-equipped conference rooms on premises that will likely be a key piece of the hybrid work puzzle? Traditionally, they have just had one camera that is typically situated at the front and affords a view of those present in that space. Recent innovations allow the camera to focus in on individuals in that room and frame them appropriately within the shot, but industry leaders like Logitech's Scott Wharton see a huge opportunity in thinking in multiples.

Scott says the real pain point is figuring out how to look at other things in the room beyond the bowling alley view: "People try to solve it with one camera, but it would be like watching a sporting event with one camera at the top. What makes a sporting event really great to watch is you have lots of cameras with a smart director moving the shot around. So, part of our vision is you're going to have many, many cameras in a conference room. Maybe it'll be 100 at some point so you can always get the best shot."

Many large conference rooms are already equipped with multiple microphone pods, so everyone can be heard clearly in the room no matter where they're seated. What about extending the video? Scott suggests, "What about video expansion cameras?"

That might mean a camera at the front to capture the entire room (the audience), a camera that can focus on the presenter who may be standing in front of that room and would possibly be seen only from the back in the bowling alley scenario, plus a nondigital camera for whiteboards so that content can be shown in an integrated way. And that would be just the beginning.

People Driving Technology Driving People

Beyond the meeting mechanics, though, much of the deeper-level discussions around meetings are focused on one goal – making meetings more productive and effective rather than just calendar-filling events. To some, achieving this goal may lie in the technology itself.

In this, Massimo Rapparini, CIO at Logitech, sees a new frontier: "When it comes to innovation and how meetings can drive innovation, I think there's a whole greenfield of opportunity. How do you do that? Do you measure people's inputs? Do you measure people's outputs? Do you figure out how people collaborate and what's the optimal environment that they can collaborate in? How do you use technology to uncover insights that allow people to be more innovative? To me, that is a blank space. We haven't really cracked that code and I think there's a big opportunity for all companies."

People adopt technology to make their meetings better. Technology is created to spawn more collaboration and creativity within the groups that use it. Perhaps that's where the future of meetings lies – at the intersection of technological innovation and best practices of meeting science. Leveraging both may allow every business to prepare for whatever is "suddenly" next.

Conclusion

Looking back and looking ahead can inform what you do today to make your meetings as effective as possible. With a near guarantee that there will be a remote component to many meetings for the foreseeable future, it's wise to flex and adapt using the new best practices we've shared. Technological innovation may result in vast improvements in our meeting experiences, but don't discount the human factor. It's dangerous to ignore the old best practices, which often trip us up, and with that, we will share some final thoughts as we conclude *Suddenly Virtual: Making Remote Meetings Work.*

Chapter Takeaways

- This book provides the knowledge and information for the starting point to make your meetings better.
- We are all human, we make good and bad habits, and we can change the bad into the good, with some effort.
- Operant conditioning, that old psychological mechanism, still applies to promoting good and eliminating bad virtual meeting behavior.
- Once we properly reflect on our virtual meeting experiences, we can engage in the Adaptive Improvement Model (AIM) and begin to make a lasting change for ourselves and others.
- Video communication will likely continue to be at the heart of virtual and hybrid meetings in the future but may incorporate augmented reality and even more robust solutions.
- New meeting technology may eventually be used to drive productivity and innovation.

References

Chen. 2020. "A dentist sees more cracked teeth. What's going on?" *The New York Times.* https://www.nytimes.com/2020/09/08/well/live/dentists-tooth-teeth-cracks-fractures-coronavirus-stress-grinding.html.

Gillihan, Seth J. 2015. "Why is it so easy to slip back into bad habits?" *Psychology Today.* https://www.psychologytoday.com/us/blog/think-act-be/201511/why-is-it-so-easy-slip-back-bad-habits.

Mroz, Joseph E., and Joseph A. Allen. 2020. "To excuse or not to excuse: Effect of explanation type and provision on reactions to a workplace behavioral transgression." *Journal of Business and Psychology* 35 (2): 187–201.

Newby-Clark, Ian. 2009. "We are creatures of habit." *Psychology Today*. https://www
.psychologytoday.com/us/blog/creatures-habit/200907/we-are-creatures-habit.

Shortsleeve, Cassie. 2018. "5 science-approved ways to break a bad habit." *Time*.
https://time.com/5373528/break-bad-habit-science/.

Thompson, Clive. 2020. "What if working from home goes on...forever?" *The
New York Times*. https://www.nytimes.com/interactive/2020/06/09/magazine/
remote-work-covid.html.

Yoerger, M., J. Crowe, M. Harms, J. Allen, and N. Lehmann-Willenbrock. 2017.
"Humor styles: How impression management influences meeting satisfaction."
Society for Industrial and Organizational Psychology Conference, Orlando, FL.

Conclusion: Our Own Remote Work Experiment

B elieve it or not, Joe and Karin have never met in person – ever. This surprising fact only came to light when one of our spouses brought up the irony that we were writing a book on a subject that we were living out in real time. Our working relationship has been and continues to be a purely virtual one.

As you may recall, the genesis of our collaboration was virtual – the webinar back in March 2020 where we appeared as subject matter experts and panelists discussing the "modern meeting," a fortuitous topic given the timing. Our planning sessions were done synchronously via videoconferencing and asynchronously using Google Docs. We're told the webinar is still getting significant traction as an *interesting* subject that became an *essential* one.

The months that followed kept both of us very busy – Joe jumped into research and consulting, while Karin and her team strove to handle the calls for help in navigating corporate communication with video at its core. The germination of the book happened over email, as we both realized the potential for bringing the Meeting Scientist Perspective and the On-Camera Coach Perspective together. Virtual meetings and the remote work that required them are not going away, and businesses need guidance, beyond gut feelings, on how to make remote meetings work. For Joe, it was an exciting opportunity to share his initial findings from a bevy of research designed to capture the impacts of the pandemic on the way we meet. For Karin, it was a chance to provide "color commentary" to his data-based insights, having helped thousands as they attempted to adjust and eventually warm to connecting through a lens.

If you do the math, you realize this book came together rather quickly. Recognizing the demand for answers, our book was fast-tracked so it could get into the hands of you, our readers, as quickly as possible without compromising the quality of the content. Joe and Karin spent countless hours on video calls with each other, leveraged collaborative tools for content creation, and decided to err on the side of overcommunication rather than under. A frequent sign-off for those video calls: "Talk to you ten times tomorrow!"

In short, the process of writing this book is anecdotal proof that remote meetings can work – quite well actually – and virtual collaboration can not only result in what we hope is a high-quality product but also something of real value.

Joe and Karin hope to meet in person one day – but at a time when some relationships are tenuous due to the lack of in-person interaction, their working relationship has been created, fostered, and strengthened purely via virtual means. If and when they do actually have an opportunity to shake hands, it will more likely be a hug – after all, that's what close friends and colleagues often do.

About the Authors

Karin M. Reed is the chief executive officer and chief confidence creator of Speaker Dynamics, a corporate communications training firm, featured in *Forbes*. While speaking through a webcam might be new to much of the world, Karin has been teaching business professionals how to be effective on-camera communicators for nearly a decade, translating her experience as an Emmy-award winning broadcast journalist, on-camera spokesperson, and actress into a methodology based upon the MVPs of On-Camera Success™. Her first book, *On-Camera Coach: Tools and Techniques for Business Professionals in a Video-Driven World*, was a #1 Hot New Release in Business Communications on Amazon in 2017. Karin and her team have been the chosen training partner for some of the world's most recognized companies and most respected academic institutions in the world – from Nike to Lenovo, from Duke University to the Graduate School of Business at Stanford. To learn more about Karin and her team, go to www.SpeakerDynamics.com.

Joseph A. Allen, PhD, is a professor of industrial and organizational (I/O) psychology at the University of Utah. Before he completed his doctorate in organizational science at the University of North Carolina at Charlotte (UNCC) in 2010, he received his master of arts degree in I/O psychology at UNCC in 2008 and his bachelor of science degree in psychology from Brigham Young University in 2005. His research focuses on three major areas of inquiry that include the study of workplace meetings, organizational community engagement, and occupational safety and health. He has more than 100 publications in academic outlets, another 20 under review, and many works in progress for a number of journals. He has presented over 250 papers/posters at regional and national conferences and given more than 100 invited presentations on his research. His previous academic publishing outlets include *Human Relations, Human Performance, Journal of Applied Psychology, Journal of Occupational and Organizational Psychology, Journal of Organizational Behavior, Journal of Business Psychology, American Psychologist, Accident Analysis and Prevention, Group and Organization Management*, and so on. He serves as a reviewer for various journals, including the *Journal of Organizational Behavior, Organizational Behavior and Human Decision Processes, Journal of Creative Behavior*, and *Academy of Management Journal*. He is an editorial board member for the *Journal of Business and Psychology, Group and Organization Management*, and the *European Journal of Work and Organizational Psychology*. He directs the Center for Meeting Effectiveness housed in the Rocky Mountain Center for Occupational and Environmental Health. Dr. Allen has consulted for more than 400 nonprofit and for-profit organizations, which include animal welfare organizations, human services organizations, large corporations, government entities, emergency safety and intelligence agencies, as well as retail conglomerates and external talent management firms. His research has attracted internal and external grant funding of more than $5 million since 2010. Dr. Allen can be reached at joseph.a.allen@utah.edu.

Index

275

Index

283

Index

285

Index